AF521949

YONEKO DAUGHTER OF HAPPINESS

By

YONEKO TAHARA

as told to

BERNARD PALMER

MOODY PRESS

CHICAGO

Library of Congress Cataloging in Publication Data

Tahara, Yoneko.
Yoneko, daughter of happiness.
1. Tahara, Yoneko. 2. Conversion. I. Palmer, Bernard Alvin, 1914- II. Title.
BV4935.T28A38 248'.246'0924 [B] 76-19009
ISBN 0-8024-9811-6

Second Printing, 1977

Printed in the United States of America

YONEKO

ONE

The door to our home was unlocked when I tried it. As the knob turned beneath my thumb and two fingers, panic seized me. The last three or four times when I was out with my friends from church, I had been locked out. Now, however, the windows were open and the place was ablaze with lights. I looked back at Akitoshi, who had brought me home on his bicycle.

"Pray for me," I whispered.

The entire family was in the living room. My honorable father, my two brothers, and my sister were sitting in a semicircle on the tatami mats, facing the door. They stared grimly at me. For the first time since I had thrown myself under a train more than a year before in a futile attempt to end my life, there was no pity, no hurt, in my father's blazing eyes. He ignored my amputated legs, my missing left arm, and the thumb and two fingers that remained on my right hand.

He had always disapproved of my newfound faith in Jesus Christ and my association with Americans, but in those months of agony following my attempted suicide he had been so grateful for the return of my smile and my renewed interest in living that he had said nothing. Now the situation had reached the place where he had to act.

Were I a proper eighteen-year-old Japanese girl in proper subjection to my father, I would not have given up the religion of my people to receive Jesus Christ. I would not have allowed my new Christian friend, Akitoshi Tahara, to take me to the meetings those cursed Americans were holding. I would have resisted their efforts to get me out on the street, bringing shame to my father and my family by handing out tracts and telling others what Christ had done for me.

I spoke to my father in a quavering voice and tried to smile. There was no sign of recognition in his face. It was as though he neither saw nor heard me. Akitoshi hesitated at the door, reluctant to leave me alone to face them. One of my brothers strode forward angrily and slammed the door, shutting the scene from my friend's uneasy eyes.

"Come here, Yoneko," Father ordered sternly in a tone that was not to be disobeyed. "Sit in the middle."

I did as I was told, although I had never before experienced anything like this. My very being trembled. It was obvious my father had more to say, but he was silent for at least a minute. I waited, praying in desperation.

"It is very important, this thing we are going to talk with you about," he said sternly. "We have been patient far too long, thinking you would come to your senses and forget this Western God. We have finally decided we can wait no longer. You must forsake this Christian religion!"

I gasped loudly enough for all of them to hear. I had suspected the purpose for the family meeting; but until he put it into words, I did not realize how poorly prepared I was for the confrontation. What would I do if they ordered me to renounce Christ or leave? I couldn't get a job to support myself. I couldn't even look after my own needs at home. Sweat moistened my forehead, and I wiped it away with my hand.

"I have decided you should stay away from this Christian religion," he continued. "It is causing trouble in this house. It is tearing our family apart. You cannot go back! You cannot go to those services anymore!" There was more anger in his voice than I had ever heard before, even when he had argued with my brothers about money for college. "You cannot let any of those terrible people into our home again!"

I looked at each of them in turn, stunned by the hatred I

read in their eyes. They had never been so united against me before. I was heartsick and desolate.

I waited for him to say more, but he had finished. He had delivered his edict. Now it would be my turn to talk. I was not sure what he expected of me. My brothers were convinced I would yield before such pressure. They were eyeing me confidently, waiting to hear me acknowledge my error and promise to give up my Christian friends and the services at church.

But they did not know me well. Rather, they did not know the keeping power of my God. A moment before a terrible fear had seized me as I considered the very real possibility that I might be faced with renouncing Christ or being turned out in the street. Now I was engulfed by a strange peace. The trembling ceased, and I was calm and relaxed.

I was actually glad they were confronting me. In my own feeble way I had been trying to witness to my family but had never been able to say more than a few words to them about Jesus Christ—words so timidly spoken they dropped on unhearing ears. Now I had an opportunity to share what I believed. At that moment I was grateful for it, but I did not know what lay ahead for me!

"You know I love all of you very much, Father," I began seriously. "It hurts me deeply to feel your disapproval after everything you all have done for me. But if you take God away from me, I will have nothing. He has saved me and has given me reason to live again. I cannot even think of what my life would be like without Him."

They were stunned by what I was saying. They expected nothing less than total victory. With the entire family facing me, united in their stand against my new religion, they were sure I would give up my faith. They could not conceive of Christ meaning so much to me.

By this time I was crying. Our culture frowns on such a display of emotion; and my father and brothers were embarrassed by it, as though it was one more indication that I had taken leave of my senses. However, I could not hold back my tears. They streamed down my cheeks, and my shoulders shook. It was several minutes before I could control myself well enough to continue.

"In spite of everything you have told me," I went on as respectfully as I could, "I am happy that I am a Christian. I know I would be damned if the Lord had not saved me. I would not even be alive if it were not for Jesus Christ. I would have taken my life when I was still in the hospital. So, if I must decide between leaving my home and all of you or forsaking my God, I—I will have no other choice than to follow Him. I belong to Christ."

They were astonished by my decision, struck silent by the words I had spoken. My stand was far different than they expected it to be. It was not that I was suddenly so brave. My own courage wilted before their hard eyes. But God had taken over. I was scarcely conscious that I was even involved.

"How can you associate with Americans?" Yasuzo demanded when he was once more able to find words to express his anger. "You know what they did at Hiroshima. How does it look to our neighbors to see that woman come here as though she is a friend of all of us?"

Akiyoshi took up the challenge, his violent temper heating his voice and hurling the words at me. "You let this American woman put you in a wheelchair and take you around town to all of your old friends so you can bring shame to us and yourself by talking with them about this Christ of yours."

Now my brothers both began to argue with me. Their reasoning poured out in a bitter torrent. "And you go out on the street corners with these people, passing out your silly pieces of paper and telling everyone that the ways of your family are not good enough, that you have forsaken us and the customs of our people and have become a Christian."

"Don't you see, Yoneko?" my oldest brother, Yasuzo, continued. "You're only being used by these people. They pretend to be kind and good and say they love you, but they don't. Their kindness is only on their lips. It does not come from the heart. They are only trying to get something from us; and when they get it, they'll be through with you."

Father, who had remained silent since I told them Christ had to have first place in my life, nodded his agreement. "What your brothers are saying is true. They want to use you to make money. They want people to feel sorry for you and give them money out of pity. When they have finished using you, it will be as Yasuzo says. They will throw you aside."

"They have never collected money on the street," I protested.

That seemed to shake him. He knew I would not lie to him, even about so important a matter. "There has to be some reason for them to be nice to you."

"It is because of Jesus Christ," I murmured.

But no one heard me. Yasuzo and Akiyoshi were both shouting at once—loud, threatening arguments designed to frighten me into doing what reason failed to accomplish. If that was their purpose, they succeeded well. I was afraid of them. Praying for strength, I spoke again.

"I only want for you what I have found," I stammered. "I only want you to have the same happiness Christ has given to me."

Their eyes were hot with anger, and their ears as unhearing as stone.

Akiyoshi was the one who acted. Arms quivering with stress, he took a long step forward and slapped me. His open hand exploded against my cheek, almost knocking me over. Stunned, I was slow in pushing myself upright once more.

The others in the room were as shocked as I was. He had slapped me before during the same sort of argument, but never in front of our father.

Hesitantly I raised my remaining hand. With my two fingers I felt the livid imprint of Akiyoshi's hand on my cheek. Father's silence indicated approval. The hurt of the blow was as nothing compared to the pain in my heart!

My name is Yoneko—rice child—daughter of happiness. My mother's mother named me, choosing one of the old names that carried the wish and the prayer that I would be well cared for all my life. To our people, the choosing of a name is not to be done hastily. The old ones believe a name has the power to influence a life.

"Yoneko," my grandmother said without emotion. "That is a name that will serve her well and help her to survive to the venerable age of eighty-eight."

I was happy enough as a child, but it was not happiness I brought to my honorable father, my sister, and my two brothers. Had I committed suicide neatly, there would have been a time of grieving softened by the fact that I had faced death in a calm, courageous manner.

But I had not.

I had been in such turmoil that night at the railway station in Tokyo that I could not think with clarity. All that mattered to me was putting an end to my useless, miserable existence. The train should have accomplished my purpose, but it only succeeded in mangling my body. Both legs were gone below the knees, while my left arm and two fingers on my right hand were amputated.

I must explain why I was so disillusioned and miserable that I longed for death. It was not the nature of our family to be sad. There was much happiness in our home when I was small, and I was a joyful child.

"Yoneko," the family would say approvingly. "Grandmother named her well."

And Grandmother would allow a thin, satisfied smile to warm the tranquility of her seamed face.

They tell me I was always anxious to help my parents, even when I was too young to go to school. That must have seemed strange to everyone. I was completely undisciplined. My mother asked me only to do the most simple of tasks, such as cleaning the front porch every day. My elder sister, Yuriko, was given far more responsibilities and was disciplined regularly. I was Mother's baby. She did not think I could be expected to mind or help with the work the way others did. And she took me with her everywhere.

"Your daughter is very beautiful," people would tell her in the shops.

"No," she would reply, pride beaming in her smile and denying her negative answer. "Your daughter is certainly pretty, but mine isn't."

And those who heard her knew that she agreed with the speaker and only said what she did out of politeness and the desire to appear to be kind and humble. My father did not like to hear such things, and a few times he grumbled his protest. Mother brushed aside his objections without ever allowing the words to register in her mind. She was a dutiful Japanese wife, accustomed to obeying his slightest wish, but I was so special to her that she could not understand anyone finding fault with anything about me.

"Can we help it that she is so beautiful?" she countered.

"It is more important to be beautiful within."

Still, he could not get her to understand that she should correct me.

I did not even have to eat at home if I didn't want to. There was a boy about my age who lived across the street. We played together constantly and were in and out of each other's homes a dozen times a day. If I came into the kitchen and saw my mother was preparing a dish that didn't quite suit my fickle taste at the moment, or if I changed my mind half-way through the meal, I would run across the street to see what my friend was having for lunch. If his food pleased me more than the food at home, I would finish eating with them. I cannot remember my mother ever scolding me for such naughtiness.

I soon learned I could get my own way anywhere in the neighborhood. I had only to sob out my troubles to Mother. If I squabbled with a friend, I could run home crying; and she would leap to my rescue like a she bear defending her cub. As far as she was concerned, I could do no wrong.

Someone had hurt me, and she would not permit that. I could not begin to count the number of times she took me by the hand and marched me to the home of my antagonist of the day to win the battle for me.

I don't recall too much about it, but with such protection and indulgence I must have been insufferable. Still, for all of that, I wanted to please my parents and was always doing things for them without being asked.

As soon as I saw my father coming back to the house in the evening after a day at work, I would run to the kitchen for his ashtray. His movements at night were always the same. He would pause at the door long enough to greet my mother and exchange his shoes for the slippers she brought him.

Ours was not the casual greeting of an American home. It was formal, a tradition from the past. The custom has already changed much as younger homes have been subjected to the influence of Western ways, but our home was as unmovable as Mount Fuji or the ocean that surrounds our islands.

Mother would bow slightly. "Welcome home."

Then she took his briefcase and anything else he was carrying and handed him his slippers so he could put them on in place of his shoes.

"The *ofuro** is ready, or would you care to eat or have a drink first?"

I waited nearby, knowing this routine was not to be interrupted. Then I held out a ceramic dish to him, steadying it with both chubby hands.

A faint, emotionless smile flecked his face in recognition of me and my contribution to his enjoyment. The well-bred Japanese reflected only peace and tranquility, as our culture for centuries has dictated. That was especially true of one like Father who had one foot in the past and the other only half in the present.

Even yet I have never heard him say he loves me. I have never had him take me in his arms and kiss me. Such a vulgar display of emotion would cause him to lose face before his family. He gestured toward the pillow on the floor that was reserved for him. It marked the place of honor that was his because of his position as the head of the house. His father before him had been accorded such respect in his home. Now it fell to him. Later his sons would be treated with the same honor by their families.

"Take it over there, please," he told me. Although his voice was carefully controlled as befit his position, I knew by the tenderness that he loved me. And, instinctively, I loved him. That was why I wanted to do nice things for him like bringing him his ashtray.

Mother's dark eyes followed me with approval as I put the tray on the tatami mat near the place where he would sit and have a smoke before dinner. When the evening meal was ready, our family seated ourselves about the low table.

There was an order to our seating arrangement that never

*Japanese bath.

varied. Father was at the head of the table in the place of honor. Mother was at the end closest to the kitchen so she could serve the rest of the family. Yasuzo, the oldest son, was beside Father. His was the most important place among the children. Akiyoshi was next to him, and then came Yuriko and I. Being girls, we did not count for much in the scheme of things.

Mother put a piece of fish on my plate. My nose wrinkled in distaste as I looked down at it. We did not often have fish, but even then we had it more than I liked.

"Will you take the bones out for me?" I asked our father.

He took my plate and with his chopsticks cut the fish into small pieces so he could remove the bones. I squirmed impatiently, waiting for him to finish.

"What is the matter, Yoneko?" Akiyoshi wanted to know. He was younger than Yasuzo by two years. Although he was still in high school, he seemed like a man to me, as big and as old and as wise and as important as our father. "Are you afraid Father will eat your fish for you, too?"

I ignored the teasing. With two older brothers, I had grown accustomed to it. "Did you get all the bones, Father?" I asked.

"I got them all," he told me. "You won't have to be afraid of getting one in your throat."

"Did you even get the little bones?"

"Even the little ones."

"Yoneko will never be able to get married," Yuriko said. "She will have to stay with Father all her life so he can take the bones out of her fish."

"Perhaps he can teach her husband to do it for her," Yasuzo said.

"When I get married, I won't eat fish," I retorted.

"You'll have to eat fish," Akiyoshi informed me. "Father is arranging a marriage for you with the son of a fishmonger."

My cheeks flamed. "I will arrange my own marriage!"

Mother's eyelids narrowed in hostility but not at me. Her displeasure was reserved for Akiyoshi. Still, she did not speak. It was Father's place to order my brothers to silence. He was the head of the house. But he handed my plate back to me without a word, as though he had heard nothing that was said.

TWO

Father and I loved each other, but we did not have the closeness Mother and I enjoyed. I knew him as a person who was away most of the time. He left the house before I was awake in the morning and came back after school was out at night.

He seldom talked with me; and when he did, he showed little interest in my friends or school. However, I did not find that disturbing. Like most Japanese men, he was reserved, ruling his wife and children with a gentle autocracy the way his father had ruled in his home.

It was not often that he talked at length with anyone in the family unless it was my brothers. Yasuzo was his first-born son and in an honored position in our home, so he was favored by Father's primary attention. Akiyoshi was his second son and, as such, was held in only slightly less esteem.

My older brother was one of those who was good at books and longed to go on to college when he finished high school. There was much discussion about it around home. I was too young to know exactly what the talking was about, but I had already learned to read the faces of my family. Whenever the matter of college came up, Father got angry. It frightened me.

"All I want to do is to go on to college next year," Yasuzo was protesting. A certain helplessness crept into his voice.

"I know what you want!" Father's slight frame trembled at the thought of it. I was to learn later that he could be very stubborn, but as a child of five or six I did not understand. At the time I was only aware that both of them were greatly disturbed. "You think I should pay your way through school, but you can put such thoughts aside. I will give you nothing for such foolishness!"

"I do not have to have your help," my brother retorted. "I have decided I am going to school."

"That is up to you. Go, if you wish. Only do not look to me for money. I will give you nothing!"

Yasuzo's face paled to the hue of a dead fish. "Then I will go on my own."

Usually that was where the argument ended. It would have stopped this time, but Akiyoshi took it up. He was the quick-tempered one.

*"Otosan!"** he exploded. "Why are you so stubborn? Everyone knows we must have an education to get ahead these days."

Father was not used to being challenged, even by his quick-tempered son. "That is what you say."

"That is what everyone says!"

Father's eyes flashed, and I slunk over beside Mother, bewildered by what I was hearing.

"Those who say such things do so because they do not know!" Father continued, calm returning to his voice. "There is only one way to get ahead. Work hard and be honest. That will help you win the trust of people, and you will be successful and happy. You will be honored for those virtues and favored above those who do not have them. If you both do those things, you will do well without having to waste time and money by going to school."

"We have heard all of that from the day when we were smaller than Yoneko," Akiyoshi blurted with a sudden wave of his hand, as though to sweep the argument away. "And we still hear it every time Yasuzo mentions that he wants to go away to school."

*Father.

"I speak of it, *ah,*" Father snapped, "but you do not hear me. It is as though your ears are closed." A look I could not understand gleamed in his eyes, and I put Mother between myself and this bewildering anger. "You will do well if you listen. Follow my steps. Forget this foolishness and do what I have done. It is the only way to get along in this world."

My brothers stared at each other, their faces white and taut and their lips quivering. It was always so when they talked with Father about college and the money it would cost to go. And always the arguments ended in the same way. Anger stole their tongues until they could not speak.

Later I heard Yasuzo and Akiyoshi discussing the matter. Father had gone out somewhere or there would have been angry words again. I remember trembling for fear that he would come home before they finished and overhear what they were saying.

"He tells us we should follow *his* example, and we'll be as successful as he is." Scorn tainted Akiyoshi's strident voice. "I should want the kind of success he has had! The office of the City Garbage Disposal Department, putting figures on paper!" He laughed haughtily. "That is something to boast of!"

Yasuzo was more charitable. "He has worked hard at his little job and on the farm," he reminded our hot-tempered brother. "Father has saved many yen. It is something to be proud of."

"Then it should not be so hard for him to help you go to school!"

My oldest brother's eyelids narrowed. It was obvious he didn't like all the anger and heated words. He was not as quick to explode as Akiyoshi. "I am the one who will be going to college next year," he said mildly. "Why should you be so upset because he refuses to help me?"

Akiyoshi's answer was quick. "You are the firstborn, while

I am only his second son." Bitterness and jealousy stole into his voice. "If he will not help you pay the expenses for college, there is no chance that he will help me."

"Arguing will do nothing," Yasuzo said. "Father has made up his mind. To keep talking will do nothing to help."

"Ah!" The word exploded from his lips. "That is what you say now. He has made up his mind, but he can change it, too!"

There had been other arguments in the past. There were more in the future about the same subject, but nothing was accomplished. When it was time for my oldest brother to go to college, he had to work his way, earning the money for his expenses. Father did not relent and help him. He had to work and meet the entire cost on his own. So did Akiyoshi, in spite of his temper and his ready arguments.

Such problems were of no concern in my tight little world, however. I heard the quarreling as I heard the chattering of the birds in the mulberry trees when I went out to the farm with Mother, but it did not trouble me. She circumscribed my own universe with herself as the center. We were both content to have it so. From the earliest I could remember, we were someone very special to each other.

I can still feel the warmth of her strong, reassuring hand as she grasped my fingers and guided me out of the house in the direction of the railway station to take the train to the village where we used to live. I was born at the farm we would be visiting and had lived there with my family until I was three years old. Then my father got a job in Hachioji City, and we moved.

I could remember little of our days on the farm, but we went back often enough so I was acquainted with the great farmhouse that belonged to our friends. I revisited the area a few years ago, and the house was small and somewhat dingy. In my child's eyes, however, it seemed as large and as towering as Fuji. Great rooms beckoned irresistibly to my short legs, compelling them to run from one room to another to another.

Although I went to the farm more often with Mother, I got to make the trip occasionally with my father. He would put me in the little cart behind his bicycle and take me with him when he went out there to work. He had his regular job during the week and on Saturday morning. Saturday afternoon and all day Sunday he was at the farm, plowing or weeding or harvesting and caring for the silk worms. Those were exciting days for me. I was allowed to run all over the place, eating mulberries. Our yard at home was *Neko no Hitai,* as we say in Japanese, or "the size of a cat's forehead." At the farm there was space to play; and I took advantage of it, running until I was tired of running.

Mother used to keep back enough cocoons from the harvest to make silk thread and weave a certain amount of material from it. She made kimonos by hand for everyone in the family. She did not work in a factory or a shop, as some mothers did, but she was busy taking care of her family. And nothing she did was as striking as the kimonos she made. Father often held one of them in his hand, his fingers caressing the beautiful material.

"They are nice," he said. "Very nice."

That was the closest I had ever seen him come to expressing gratitude or love to her.

Mother took me with her wherever she went, even when Yuriko was at home and could have looked after me. On one particular day the two of us were going out to the farm once more. And on the way, as we usually did, we would stop at the temple near the graves of our ancestors to pay homage to them.

In most families the father was the one who was the most

religious. He was the head of the house and was charged with the responsibility of seeing that his home had a shrine and that their ancestors were properly worshiped.

My father was a second son, which meant that he would not inherit his father's business, nor would he be responsible for worshiping his ancestors. The oldest son was, by tradition, given the bulk of his father's estate and was charged with carrying on the worship of the members of the family who had died previously.

It was a custom in Japan then, and among some families even today, for a couple without children to adopt a youthful male friend or relative for the express purpose of carrying on ancestor worship. That happened to my father. He had remained at home with his parents the same as before; but when his adoptive parents died, he was given their farm. In return he was faithful in worshiping them at the *butsudan* or family shrine in our living room.

He made it plain to all of us, however, that he only carried out his duties before the shrine out of honesty and not because he believed in such activities. He had given his word that he would worship his adoptive parents in return for the farm, so he was faithful in doing so.

In our home it was Mother who rang the bell in worship before the family shrine. It was Mother who made the trips to the temple. Father did not object to that. Nor did he find fault with her friendship with the priests. He had no time for such foolishness himself, and he was glad to be relieved of the responsibility.

Father was convinced a man had to be able to see in order to believe anything. He had to handle the object of his trust with his hands and know for a certainty it was genuine, or trust could not be given. Hard work and honest dealing and frugal living were elements he understood. He knew first-hand what they could mean in a man's life. Why think about religion when it was clothed with superstition and had no practical value for anyone?

A woman with all her weaknesses might find help at the temple. He wouldn't know about that. It might even be all right for a child who had not yet learned to take care of himself, or even for a man who was creaking painfully through the final weeks or months of life. It could only be a hindrance to one who was strong and well able to take care of himself.

From other visits I knew what Mother would do once we were at the temple. We would make our way up the rough path and through the weeds that reached high on the gravestones. We would stop for a moment at the graves of our ancestors. That we always did.

We would also take oranges or a similar gift along for the family we would be visiting, an evidence of good breeding which all Japanese observed.

"We must always have a gift for those we call on," Mother would explain to me carefully, so I would tuck that important scrap of information in my mind against the day when I would be grown and making calls without her.

I knew the ritual well. When we got to the house, there would be elaborate greetings, denials of worthiness, and an invitation to come in. Then the woman of the house would take our gift to their butsudan and place it there as an offering to the departed spirits of their ancestors. Later it would be taken away and eventually used by the members of the family.

I began to see that worshiping in the temples was even more important than giving gifts when we visited friends and relatives. At least my mother placed much more importance upon it.

"Did you ever think how fortunate we are to live close enough so we can visit this temple of *Tenri-Kyo*† and not

†Shinto sect founded in Tenri City in western Japan.

have to worship always at the little one near home?" she would say to me every time we made the journey. "Here there are priests who know all about our prophet and how she had her vision and what was revealed to her. Yoneko, she was possessed by the gods and appointed to do mighty things. There is nothing more wonderful than to sit at their feet and hear of her wisdom and the power of her gods."

Distant horizons claimed Mother's gaze. Though I was so small that I could understand but little of what she said, I was overwhelmed by the awe her words inspired.

"Many times I have had my future foretold," she would say to me. "Many times I have been healed without a doctor."

Religion meant much to my mother. I have much sorrow that she did not know my Christ.

THREE

I do not know how or when my mother first got interested in Tenri-kyo, a Shinto-Buddhist sect quite widely accepted in our part of Japan. I only know that my earliest memories include regular visits to the temple and hearing the prayers and the chantings and the gongs and the drum. I remember walking through the weeds to the graves of our ancestors and then to the temple where we went regularly to worship. Most Japanese were careless in the exercising of their religion, but not Mother. She carried out every act of devotion as faithfully as she knew how.

She was also most generous, even during the war years when there was so little of everything; and the priests of that temple were close friends of hers. They would invite us into their house, and we would sit around the old farm-type fireplace built right into the floor. I remember the fire was kept going all day long, even though the weather was very hot, and I would look up at the underside of the smoke-blackened thatched roof. There was a small hole in it to let the smoke out, but there was no ceiling in the room that seemed as vast as the ocean to me. There was a shelf on the rafters to keep things dry.

After I got over my shyness, I would play around the poles that helped support the roof. I was especially fond of the largest in the center of the house, the ridgepole.

"Do you know what that pole represents, Yoneko?" the kindly priest asked me. "It is a symbol of your father's power, the strength of the money he brings to the family."

I still did not understand. He knew I wouldn't. But the day would come when the meaning would be clear to me. My mother was always asking someone to teach me or pray for me when I was ill. She would have them put their hands on me and ask the gods to heal me. She had dreams of making me a disciple and perhaps a leader, although she did not voice those hopes to me. It looked as though I was willing to follow the path she was charting for me. The other women praised her for my devotion and my quickness to learn.

"How fortunate you are," they would say. "The gods will be much pleased with Yoneko. Prosperity and health and many blessings will come to your family because of your faithfulness in working with her."

Even I was not aware of it then, but there was rebellion in my heart, a fierce desire to be independent and free. It would not show itself until after a stroke claimed Mother's life; but it was hidden there, a sleeping tiger no one knew existed. I was still the dutiful little girl doing all she wanted me to, for I longed to please her.

I learned my lessons well.

Tenri-kyo, "the religion of divine wisdom," was founded by a woman. Some of those who have been chosen to lead others have to study long years, mastering the difficult, hidden meaning of certain religious documents. Others travel endlessly across the land, visiting temples and shrines until they have earned enough favor to be trusted with the ultimate experience. But she was of a special few whose lives were so pure and holy, whose thoughts were so sublime, that they were visited by the gods without years of study or seeking. Her revelation came like lightning exploding across the nighttime sky. She did not have to earn it. It was given to her.

Some said she was possessed because the father god, the all-source god who is over several lesser gods, had taken control of her. He put her in a trance and granted her a vision that showed her his message. She was to proclaim that message to the world.

There were three promises he would make to her faithful followers. They would have good personal health, there would be peace in their families, and their business ventures would prosper. In order to earn those blessings, their faith had to be strong and they had to give money or the first of the crop to the temple. Whatever they gave was supposed to be of their best. As special gifts, the god gave her and her followers the ability to heal the sick and to tell the future.

Childlike, I accepted everything as the proper way to worship. I see now that they whip their people to a frenzy of emotion with chanting and prayers and rhythmic, trance-inducing dances to the accompaniment of bells and the drum.

There was no conflict in our home because of Mother's religion. It did not require us to take down either our butsudan or our Shinto shrine. Neither did it require any god shelf of its own. I suppose Father was glad enough for this new source of assistance. He actually had no faith in it himself; but, like most Japanese, he figured it didn't hurt for Mother to seek the rewards of new and different gods, just in case there would be one with some power.

My mother should have been among the first to receive the earthly blessings given the followers of Tenri-kyo, so great was her devotion and her generosity to her religion. It was during the terrible shortages of the later war years when getting enough to eat was a major undertaking. Father had the farm in addition to his job and worked it as carefully as though it were his only source of income. And she gave freely of his soybeans and rice and corn and vegetables. I don't know what he thought about her giving so much away, or if he ever ordered her not to do so, but she continued to share our produce with the priests and others who were in need. Before her first illness she had been made a sort of subleader and was in charge of the bell or gong. When that happened, her joy was complete.

I was fifteen when Mother had her first stroke, and a terrible fear seized me. I didn't look to her faith-healing friends, though they swarmed into the house with their chanting and laying on of hands and many prayers. I think it was then that I realized I had gone along with my mother's religion only because it pleased her.

"Your mother will get well," our neighbor who often went to the temple with us assured me. "We have prayed and chanted and rung the bell and had her drink the holy water. She is a good woman of much faith. The gods will heal her!"

I could not bring myself to believe that Mother might die. But neither could I have faith that her religion would make her well. Like my father, what little trust I had was reserved for our doctor. I hovered over her constantly, stricken with remorse that I had often grieved her by staying out at night later than I should have and because I had been careless in taking care of my clothes around the house. I would gladly have given my own life to have seen her strong and well again.

Slowly her strength came back, but her right hand and her left leg were paralyzed and would not respond to treatment. Months passed and there was no improvement. Nor could the doctor give us any hope that we would see her able to walk and take care of our home again. My heart was dead within me.

Taking care of both Mother and the house was my responsibility during those difficult weeks. My sister, Yuriko, had gone through sewing school and was working, and both of my brothers were in college. Father had not relented to help them financially, but they had found a way. Yasuzo was married.

I had to polish the wooden kitchen floor with a little rice

bran and a cloth tied to a stick, cook our breakfast of rice and salted salmon, and fix a lunch for Father to take with him of a vegetable flavored with a tiny piece of beef or pork or some broiled fish, plus white rice and tea.

I had to clean the house and fold kimonos and fix tea. And I had to put up Mother's hair in a tight little bun at the back of her head. It was very difficult for me. Not only did I have to do those things, but I had to follow her directions to the smallest detail.

"You have only brushed over the porch, Yoneko," she would say critically. "Do it again. This time clean the corners, too."

And when I fixed her hair, she was never satisfied. "No. No, no, Yoneko. That is not the way I want it. Bring it over this way—so!" She would gesture with her hand, trying to make me understand.

I would loosen her long black hair and try again, so frustrated and confused that the tears were never far away. I see now that she was not herself in those days. Always a vigorous, active woman, her mind was that way still. Only now her body would not respond. Her carping at me was a form of release, a way of fighting against her own bewilderment and hurt. However, I saw it as being directed at me; and she had never so much as raised her voice to me before. I couldn't help feeling rejected.

Then Father came home with the news that he had heard of a place they said might help her. It was a hot springs some two hundred miles from where we lived. It was supposed to do wonderful things for people who were afflicted as she was.

"I will take you and Yoneko there," he said tenderly. "You can stay as long as you feel you should."

I studied her thin face, fearful that she would believe such a trip to be a denial of her religion and refuse to go. That thought may have been in her heart. Her trust in her beloved

Tenri-kyo was strong. But she was a dutiful wife who obeyed her husband. Whatever her own feelings, we went to the springs.

We stayed in a small apartmentlike room for an entire month that summer. Mother went into the water many times a day, staying as long as she could stand the intense heat. I would go in with her; and when it got too warm for me, I would wait for her on the sidewalk. I would not have left her, even if I could. I wanted to stay close by, to be there if I was needed.

I would tie her soft straw slippers on her feet so she would not lose them as she shuffled painfully along, and put her cane in her hand. Even with the cane she had to be helped so much I was exhausted by the time we had covered the two hundred yards to the springs where she would get into the water.

All around us were people who were less crippled than Mother. I was jealous of them and resented their good fortune. Why couldn't one of them have been afflicted so severely instead of her? Why did one as good and as kind and as generous as she have to suffer so much?

I was lonely at the springs and anxious to get back home, but I was more anxious to see my mother well.

"You are getting a little better," I would say hopefully, as though expressing the thought might, in some unexplainable way, make it true.

"Hai," she would answer. "Yes. I think so."

I am sure my own fierce independence came from her. She always wanted to do things for herself, even when her paralysis was the worst.

"I can move my fingers a little."

I would wince as I watched her struggle to twitch even one finger enough so I could see the movement.

"See?"

"Hai!" I tried to put excitement in my voice, but we both knew I had seen nothing at all. It was a little charade we used to build up each other's spirits.

The day did come, however, when the warmth of the water or the minerals or Mother's determination to take care of herself again began to loosen the bonds that held her arm and leg immobile. I cried when I saw her move her afflicted hand for the first time.

After that it seemed each successive day showed a little more improvement. She could wriggle a toe and then move her ankle. Not far, for the bonds were only loosening. They hadn't yet been broken. Then her knee began to free itself. The magic was also working on her arm. Her wrist responded to her will to move, and so did her elbow and her fingers. She held out her crippled hand triumphantly.

"Look, Yoneko!" One by one she moved her fingers.

There was no need for either of us to pretend any longer. It was apparent to everyone. By the end of the month she was able to walk without my help and found it necessary to use her cane only to steady herself. It was a great victory. We were overjoyed when we went home.

Mother took renewed interest in her religion upon our return, as though the gods had, indeed, answered the petitions of her fellow believers and brought the healing to her wasted body. I did not accept her reasoning, but it did not annoy me to hear her speak of the way she had been healed. What difference did it make whether the healing waters of the spa or the ministrations of the followers of Tenri-kyo had brought about the miracle? Her health was almost totally restored. We could not ask for more.

The doctor probably could have warned us that what had happened once might be repeated suddenly and without warning. But he did not. And we all were sure that she was well and would have no more problems. It was almost two years later that tragedy struck.

Every morning since returning home Mother had gone for a walk in the neighborhood. She would go down the little hill to the park at the bottom and wander aimlessly along the narrow, winding paths until she began to tire. It was a regular routine she followed to strengthen her leg and enjoy the warm spring air.

For some reason I was disturbed when I saw her leave that morning. A vague, nameless dread depressed me, and I insisted on going with her. Usually she was glad to have my company. This particular day, however, she was determined to be alone. Still, she did not protest until we had covered half the distance to the park.

"You don't have to go any farther with me, Yoneko," she said sharply.

"You may need help," I protested.

"Nonsense. Go on back. I can manage quite nicely by myself."

Still, I did not want to leave her. It was almost as though I feared this was my last opportunity to walk with her.

"Yoneko," she repeated, frustrated by my reluctance to follow her orders, "go back home. I don't need you with me this morning. I'm going to stop here and visit my friend."

Grudgingly I left her side and started home. Mother was motionless on the path, watching me. I have often wondered since if she had a premonition that morning of what was about to happen and wanted to spare me the agony of seeing her fall, or if she was disgruntled and resented my hovering over her. I will never know.

Bewildered and a little hurt at her abrupt dismissal, I made my way up the hill without looking back. I must have covered half the distance to our home when she leaned heavily on her cane and shuffled into her friend's yard to visit. Our neighbor was a recent convert to Tenri-kyo, and she and Mother had much to talk about. She had all the zeal of one new to the faith and was aggressive in her witness. Mother found it a joy to be with her.

Then everything happened at once.

She was moving slowly toward the front door when her friend's big dog, unnoticed until that instant, charged out at her from around the corner of the house, barking wildly. No one could understand why he acted so strangely. It may have been the cane that infuriated him, or perhaps the fact that her steps were halting caused him to sense something was wrong, something that might threaten the family he protected. He knew her well; and while he barked at her once in awhile, his challenge had never been so fierce.

I heard him and wheeled, panic clutching at my throat. I didn't have to *see* what was happening. I *knew* she was in serious difficulty. The dog half-crouched between her and the house. His savage barking increased in intensity. She swayed, both hands clutching the cane. Slowly her knees folded, and she collapsed on the ground. I flew down the hill and, ignoring the dog, threw myself upon her, shaking her and pleading with her to get up.

By this time the neighbors were running to us.

"Get Dr. Yenai!" I screamed. "Somebody call Dr. Yenai!"

"No!" Mother's friend ordered with crisp authority. "That will ruin everything! We have this holy water. It has been blessed by the priests. If she drinks it, she will be well!"

I had seen Mother like that before: the color gone from her face, her eyes closed, her breathing heavy and labored. As young as I was, I realized she had had another stroke.

"Call the doctor for me," I pleaded. "Please! Somebody call Dr. Yenai!"

One of the women started to go for the doctor, but the

woman Mother was going to visit was furious. She blocked the way.

"If you call the doctor, you will be responsible for her death. She is a good woman of much faith. The gods will heal her!"

Brusquely, she pushed me aside and knelt, taking Mother's head in her lap. "Drink this," she murmured, as though Mother could hear her. "Drink just a little and you will be all right. That's it. *Ah!* Yoneko, did you see? She drank it. The gods will heal her and give her a long life and much happiness."

I was numb and dead inside. She had poured some of the water between Mother's lips, and it dribbled down her chin, but I had not seen even so much as a drop go into her mouth.

Had I been a little older or a little more certain of myself, I would have called Dr. Yenai in spite of the angered protestations of our neighbor. I wanted to get my father. He would know what to do. But it was impossible. He had gone to work, and I didn't know how to reach him.

Mother's friend was content to have her lie in the yard where she had fallen, confident that at any instant she would open her eyes, get to her feet, and come inside for tea. A certain excitement gripped her, as though we would soon see a miracle that could be credited to Tenri-kyo and would win over even those who scoffed.

However, I could not see Mother lying helplessly on the ground. I borrowed a sliding door from someone, the kind that is used to close the house for the night, and carefully we placed her on it, taking her inside. Finally, late in the afternoon I could stand it no longer. Without saying anything to anyone, I left the house and phoned our family doctor. He came immediately.

"It is almost too late," he said, examining her gravely. "It is a very serious case. I should have been called hours ago."

He got some men to carry her up the hill to our home and told us to expect the worst. "Even if I had been called immediately, it would have been difficult to save her. As it is—" He gestured helplessly.

For three days I sat beside Mother's bed, not caring whether I ate or slept. Father was there, too, staring at her and saying little. I knew she wasn't going to get well, that I would never hear her voice again. I overheard the doctor talking with Father and Yasuzo and his wife, whispering to each other and to my older sister. But I think I would have known anyway. I think I knew from the instant I heard the dog bark and saw her fall.

Father told me I should go back to school after missing two or three days. She might lie this way for some time, he said. He would stay with her and see that she had what she needed. I didn't want to leave her, but the thought of arguing with him did not occur to me. He told me what I should do. I did it.

That afternoon I had a phone call at school telling me to come home. Nothing more. I needed no other message. Mother had died.

The neighbors who were members of Tenri-kyo and were Mother's best friends were bitter about her death. "It proves she didn't have the faith she pretended to have," they said to each other. "She deceived us, but she couldn't deceive the gods."

"She was generous," one of the group remarked. "During the war she shared what she had with us."

"That must have been to earn favor for herself. The gods counted it as dust."

They didn't come to see us, nor would they speak when we met on the street. Mother had violated their glorious religion by dying of a stroke when everyone knew the faithful would be healed. It was her own fault her health had not been restored. Deep within her heart she must not have trusted the gods enough, so they withheld the blessing of a restored body.

They did not say such things to us, but we heard them all the same. Friends came to us with their murmurings, their voiced anger against our mother.

As for me, their words meant nothing. A great void overwhelmed me. I had not realized how much Mother meant to me and how much I would miss her. Now life was not worth living. It was empty. Meaningless. And I had only contempt for Tenri-kyo. All religion was a farce!

FOUR

The coming weeks and months were a blur to me, a night-mare of agony. I was as one without a mind, without feelings and without a soul. I went to school. I came home. I went out with my friends and stayed so late and did things that caused Yuriko to worry. She scolded me frequently, but I paid no attention to her.

I had not visited bars and stayed out half the night and run around with friends and been so wild and uncontrollable until after my mother died. I would not admit it, even to myself, but I was only trying to forget. Still, I could feel the razor edge of grief turning in my heart as painfully as it had that terrible morning when I came flying down the hill and knelt beside her motionless form.

As I rode the train late one February night, a strange nervousness unsettled me. We should be nearing the famed amusement center on the beach that had been providing recreation for all of Tokyo since long before I was born. We had been traveling far enough to have been there by this time, but the train was rocketing over the rails without slackening its pace. I glanced at my watch once more, so confused I didn't notice the time, and then twisted halfway around in the seat. It was useless trying to make out a familiar landmark in the moon-washed blur of homes and streets that were racing by. I could see nothing I recognized.

Nausea wrung me limp and my very being trembled. There was no doubt now as to what had happened. I had done it again. Born and raised in greater Tokyo, I knew the transit system as well as I knew the way about my own neighborhood. Still, I was on the wrong train for the third or fourth time that same night.

I had already decided what I would do. The determination had been growing in my mind. Actually, I had planned this all along. That was the reason I had been so concerned about getting to the beach.

Once I arrived at the ocean I would lay aside my coat and my skates so that my family would know where I had gone and what had happened to me. In my confusion and misery I thought that would be enough to ease their hurt. I would walk out into the water then. I would walk and walk and walk. With every step I would shout my anguish and frustration and bitterness, flinging pain and anger at the wind until the undertow would mercifully jerk me into the warm, obliterating womb of the sea where I would suffer no more.

After I had accepted the fact that I was going to take my life, a grim excitement controlled me. I had to get back to the railway terminal and out to the amusement park on the ocean as quickly as possible. There I could carry out my plans to bring an end to this nightmare that was my life.

Sitting alone on the train, I tried to remember how many trains I had ridden that terrible evening, how many times I had realized I was in error after leaving the main terminal and had retraced my steps, but I could not. And I still was not on the train I should have taken. I turned back slowly to stare at the empty seats and the closed doors across from me. All was blurred into one numbing whirl of noise and bewilderment and loneliness. It was as though I had been on the train for most of my lifetime and was doomed to ride it helplessly into eternity.

"Yoneko." I repeated my name in a hoarse whisper, as though I might forget who I was and in doing so lose all touch with reality.

Yoneko. My grandmother had named me. The name she chose carried with it the prayer that I would be well cared for all my life and would survive to the venerable age of eighty-eight.

The first wish had already come true for me. My father had pushed aside his own grief at the death of my mother and tried to buy happiness for me. But there was no lasting satisfaction in the things he bought. My life was as empty and as purposeless as ever.

The second wish, far from bringing comfort, was frightening. It was a sentence, a block of stone fastened to my neck with one hundred kilos of forged chain that I had to drag with me. Why would anyone want to live to be eighty-eight years old? I could not even bear the thought of enduring another tomorrow!

The only other person I could see, except for the conductor in his cubicle at the front of the car, was a local commuter sprawled wearily on the worn cushions, his tired eyes closed against the dim light. As the train braked for another station, he stirred; and I realized he had not been asleep at all.

Self-consciously I wondered if he had heard me repeating my name aloud and what he was thinking if he had. It was not probable that my voice had carried above the noise of the rails, but I was in such turmoil I could not be sure. I could not be sure about anything anymore.

The commuter looked at me with narrowed eyes, questions crinkling his forehead. Briefly his gaze shifted from my oval face to the ice skates flung over my shoulder. I knew what he was thinking. Not many girls had shoe skates that cost as many yen as a man's watch or a coat from one of the better shops. He was wondering how I got the money for them. And if I were a nice girl, what was I doing out alone so late at night?

I felt an almost overwhelming compulsion to explain that my father had gotten them for me, and I was out so late because I could not bear the thought of being at home alone. I wouldn't be on the train now, but my muddled mind refused to function as it should. I could not even find the right train to take me where I wanted to go.

Although I felt the need to explain the skates and my being out so late, I made no move to do so. What I did or didn't do was no concern of his, I told myself.

"Your station?" he asked.

I saw, then, that he was reading one of the pornographic magazines the men often bought to read on the trains but would not take home with them. He looked up and I squirmed under his lustful gaze. Anger, hot as lava, seared its way to the depths of my soul.

"Your station?" he repeated.

I do not remember what I said to him, or if I spoke at all. I only know I left the train as though in a trance and stood, helpless and alone, on the empty platform until the red lights on the rear of the last coach disappeared. I was glad the man with his dreadful eyes had gone on.

What was happening? Was I losing my mind?

If I had taken more than a single pint of beer that afternoon I might have concluded it was the alcohol that had dulled my senses. But I didn't even have that to blame for my confusion. My friends, quite drunk by the time they decided to go home, had left me outside the bar hours before. Any effect the beer may have had would have long since been gone.

For a moment I surveyed the situation. If I was to go to the beach, I would have to retrace my steps to the main terminal and try once more to locate the train that went there.

I noted the schedule on the board. There would be a somewhat lengthy wait before I could get another train to take me back to the terminal. The last commuters were already home; and the schedules, geared to the rush hours, listed only a few trains at night.

I moved uneasily to the outer rim of the platform, shivering in the frigid winter wind. The city below was slumbering peacefully. *What would it be like to rest again?* I wondered. *How would it feel to sleep without dreams and to awaken without a frozen chunk of lead in my stomach?*

The turmoil of the day still imprisoned me, confusion building on confusion until I was so bewildered that I could not separate the events—even now I can't. The afternoon was a jumble of jostling crowds and trains that never went where I wanted to go.

I might have been able to excuse myself for getting on the wrong train the first time, although it had never happened before. I had been caught in the crush of homebound workers and was carried passively into the crowded coach.

After two or three stops, I had realized my mistake and gotten off. The hour was still early, and trains were coming and going every few minutes, but I was so confused I did not think about getting back to the terminal immediately. I went to the platform railing and, leaning wearily on it, looked out over the homes and streets that surrounded the station.

Most of the houses were lighted at least in one room, and the street lights glowed at each intersection, but a brilliant winter moon dwarfted their effectiveness. The roof of a car parked not far away gleamed like polished silver. At first the effect was startling. Then I saw the car was grabbing the pale shaft of light from the moon and flinging it at me.

I could not quite understand why there was no one moving about on the streets below. Even the cab drivers had quit cruising for business until morning.

I left the station platform and made my way down the cold concrete steps to the street. I heard another train leaving the station above for the main terminal. Dimly I realized I should have been on it, but that was only slightly disturbing. What did it matter what time I got back, or if I got back at all? Nobody cared.

Crossing the street, I was as one in a dream, forcing myself to walk without any awareness of moving. There were a few shops in the area, scattered among the homes. I stopped and looked in one or two, trying to spark an interest that wasn't there. Even in the moonlight that was half as bright as day I saw nothing. My eyes were awake, but my mind was not functioning.

The feeling of loneliness crept in on me as it had for weeks. It pried insidiously into my inner thoughts, wrapping its icy coils about every waking moment. I had never known such loneliness. I was the only person left in all the world. There was no one to talk to—no one to care. I was alone—completely and totally alone.

Having my mother die had been a hard enough blow, but my despair had grown worse after my closest friend betrayed me. I had been so desperate to find someone who would understand me that I had opened my anguished soul to her, telling her things I had never shared with anyone else. I was sure I could trust her not to repeat anything I told her.

But she did. For reasons I still do not comprehend, she spread the story wherever she went. It came back to me a dozen times, twisted and exaggerated until I could scarcely recognize it.

I know better than to put my trust in people now, but I had not learned that bitter lesson then, and I was crushed. If I could not trust her, I thought, I could not trust anyone. In that moment an even greater emptiness staggered me.

I did not know why I was singled out for such agony or

why I should have everyone turn against me. For a moment I was even angry with my mother, as though her dying had been part of a plot against me.

I thought I could trust my father, but he and my older brother busied themselves with arrangements for my marriage. Yuriko, my sister, had fallen in love and was engaged. Father had no objection to that. But with me it was different. He did not trust me well enough to allow me the same privilege, as though I would choose someone who would bring unhappiness to me and shame to our family.

I knew what he was thinking. He had voiced his reasoning to me. What could an inexperienced, frivolous girl know of judging character? How would I be able to weigh the reputation of a prospective husband's family in such a way as to bring honor to myself and our family name?

I realize now that finding a husband for me was only one more fumbling attempt to help me get over Mother's death. At the time, however, I looked at it as an effort to rid himself of the responsibility of taking care of me. It was yet another indication that I was being rejected by my family.

When I had trusted my best friend and she betrayed me, that finished it. I felt that there was no one who loved me, no one I could trust and confide in. I was only a shell that talked and moved and occupied space. The real Yoneko did not exist anymore.

All of those thoughts raced through my mind as I paced the streets, trying to sort out the tangled threads of reasoning. At last, numbly, I turned back toward the station. As I neared the car with the moon reflecting off its roof, all my grief and bewilderment and loneliness exploded within. What caused that reflection to crush me with despair I did not know. Even now I cannot explain it, but suddenly I was overwhelmed. I could fight no longer. The time had come when I had to act. Whatever else happened, I *had* to get to the ocean that night!

My teachers would not be too surprised when they saw the newspapers. I had gone to them several times in an effort to learn the meaning of life, but they had no help to offer.

"It is not good to be concerned about such matters," I was told. "You should be more serious about your studies so you'll get better grades. You are thinking too deeply. That is why you do not get good grades in certain subjects. Do not be burdened about life and death. Put those things out of your mind. Forget about them."

There was one who was more anxious to help than the others; but he, too, was lacking in thoughts that could quiet my aching heart.

"It is foolish for a pretty girl like you to disturb herself with problems that cannot be resolved," he said. "The greatest thinkers of the world have wrestled with those matters and were defeated. You must forget such things. Keep finding new interests to keep you busy so you will not allow yourself to be troubled. Enjoy the years that are ahead of you."

I listened to all of them and tried to do as they advised. All of my teachers were so sure they were right and were so quick with words that, at times when I was talking with them, I thought they were giving me the help I sought. Later I realized their thinking was as empty and as frustrated as my own. I was to do as they had done, cutting off my thoughts as the roots of the bonsai tree were cut to keep it small enough for the table.

Although they were my teachers and were wise in many things, I could not follow their urging in the matters of life and death. There had to be an answer somewhere, I decided. If only I could find it, I might be able to piece my miserable life together and go on. If I could not, it would not be worth living.

I wished my mother's uncle had not died. Our family had never been close to him, and I had not seen him often; but when I was a little girl, he gave me two books that meant much to me.

For a long while he had been a Roman Catholic priest in Tachikawa City, ten miles or so from our home. Finally, he quit, for a reason that was never told to me, and got married.

I do not know whether he could have helped or not, but often, when I was so troubled I could not sleep, I wished I could have talked to him.

If I had listened to my father, though, I would not have considered talking to anyone about religion. He had the same thoughts as my teachers. According to them, religion was nothing. Science and man were everything.

"You should study philosophy from the ancient writings of the greatest thinkers of the world," one of my instructors told me.

"Explore the work of more modern authors," one of the others advised. "Modern philosophers do not have the problem of protecting the old religious beliefs of our people. They will come closer to revealing the truth."

Not knowing which was correct, I had taken the advice of both. For the next several weeks I had buried myself in the writings of Japan's most outstanding philosophers, along with Johann von Goethe and others, poring over everything I could find.

One book that intrigued me above all others was simply entitled *On Suicide.* It was a small paperback that could be carried in a pocket. You would have to know my country and our people to understand such a book. It delves into the philosophy of suicide and the thinking that leads individuals to take their own lives. I was fascinated; and when I finished reading it, I went on to other books that considered different aspects of the subject. I wanted to learn the truth, to come upon the writings of someone who might have the answers to my problems. Some of the writers included teachings from the Bible. They, too, were sincere seekers and wrote according to their knowledge. I read and read in the hope that somehow, somewhere, I would find someone who could give me the answers to life.

But in all of my reading I found no help anywhere for my doubts and fears, and no answer to the questions that tormented me. There was no peace for my troubled heart nor purpose for my life.

In the first confusing years of my teens I had started a diary, recording the innermost thoughts and desires that were so important to me then. It was a habit I still continued. Only now it took a new turn. I began to write poetry, as sad and questioning and empty as my own life.

> I envy the birds
> They are so free
> They can go anywhere they want to go
> But I can't express myself as freely as they can.
> Why am I so limited and bound?
> Why don't I have the joy and happiness they seem to have?
> Why can't I enjoy life the way they seem to?

I was not aware of it at the time, but I had already traveled far down the road from which there could be no turning back. My thoughts went inward until all the little world I knew revolved around myself. It became increasingly obvious that there was only one way out of my grief and meaningless existence.

I was not quite ready for that, however.

Although my friends were not aware of it, I sought help from them. There was no special boyfriend in my life, but I was popular enough so there was always someone around to take me places. Whenever I had the chance, I talked with them about serious matters like the purpose of life and death. I was disappointed in their replies. They were even less helpful than my teachers and my family. All that concerned them was having a good time.

We played tennis and skated and danced and visited the bars. We laughed a lot and tried to make ourselves believe we were having a good time. I didn't ask anyone else, so I don't know what they thought about it, but I had discovered there was nothing enjoyable about the frantic rush of activities. I tried, deliberately, to get myself so exhausted that I would be able to sleep at night. On occasion that happened. More often it did not. By this time I had skidded even deeper into the black abyss of dejection.

Back at the railway terminal that fateful night, I went over the timetable once more, checking it carefully. That should not have been necessary. I knew which train I was to take. I had ridden it often enough in calmer, happier days. Only now I could not trust myself. There was something wrong that caused me to do strange things.

Even though I knew how to get to the Amusement Center as well as I knew how to find my way along the street where we lived, I once more got on the wrong train.

From that moment I was so disoriented that I do not know what happened next. I had at least one more false start out of Shinjuku, the train terminal. There may have been more. How many other wrong trains I got on, how many other mistakes I made, I do not know. Only God had followed my steps with certainty during those awful hours.

There was good reason for my bewilderment, but I did not know it at the time. I wouldn't have understood it if I had. There was a little evangelical church fifteen or twenty minutes enroute from Shinjuku to Enoshima and the beach. Its kindly, gray-haired pastor had been torn apart by the suicide of a young man who threw himself in front of a train at that busy terminal two years before. Every day the elderly minister prayed for those who approached the stop with suicide in mind, asking God to prevent them from destroying themselves and to bring them to a saving knowledge of Jesus Christ. I did not realize I was under the protective hand of a God I did not know, a God I would have scorned.

The watch on my wrist indicated it was almost twelve o'clock—if I dared to believe it, if I could believe anything in that jumble of dejection. That meant it was too late to catch a train to the beach. It was too late to do anything except to go home.

I was suddenly overwhelmed with the desire to get home as fast as I could. I had to get home! I had to get home! That refrain hammered through my being, blotting out all else. I could not understand this sudden compulsion or why I would want to heed it. I had spent the months since my mother's death in running, running, running so I would not have to be home with my memories. Now I felt that I could not stay away any longer. I had to get back as quickly as possible!

Mechanically I went over and checked the schedule. The trains did not go often at that time of night. I would have to wait thirty minutes to catch one that went to the end of the line where my home was located. Thirty minutes! It might as well have been eternity!

The wind nipped my ears and rubbed my cheeks raw and numb with cold. I went over to the waiting room, pulled open the door, and slipped inside. I might have stayed but there were several drunken men in the back with a couple of girls. At first I tried to ignore them. Then I went back outside.

It was even colder than before, or so it seemed. But I was so disturbed that the cold meant nothing to me. I went to the far end of the platform near a short flight of concrete steps that led down to the rails. I stood motionless for a time, oblivious to everything around me. I don't recall how long I stood there or when I sat down on the second or third step, wrapped miserably in my thoughts. I wouldn't even have known what I did if others had not told the police later.

No one would miss me if I went ahead with my plans, I decided. It would only make life simpler for the rest of my family. Father and Yasuzo would not have to concern themselves with making arrangements for a husband for me, and Yuriko could go ahead with her plans to marry. At the time I thought I was being selfless and practical. Now I realize I was swimming in self-pity and had never been more selfish.

The train was announced. I heard it stop and the doors opened. The loud speakers droned off the stops it would be making as it continued on its route.

I did not look up. I didn't have to. I knew exactly what was happening. The conductor would glance at the engineer before blowing his whistle as a final warning. The doors would close and the train would begin to move forward.

I got to my feet, still not knowing what I was about to do. The train lurched, gathering speed. Just as quickly, I stepped in front of it!

FIVE

I remember hearing the squeal of the emergency brakes on the train and the mournful wailing of the ambulance siren. As in a horrible dream, I heard myself screaming, "It hurts! It hurts!" I couldn't associate myself with the accident any more than that, and I began to wonder who was hurt.

It was strange. I recognized the voice as mine. I knew what I was crying out. Yet I was unaware that I was the one involved.

I learned later that two railroad workers (electric wire engineers, I believe we call them in Japan), were on that train going to work. They had ropes with them that they used in their jobs, and they were trained to give first aid. Before the train came to a stop, they had flung open the door and jumped out. They were the ones who dragged me from beneath the wheels of the train and used their ropes as tourniquets to stop the bleeding. They were the ones who called the ambulance. Even today I do not know their names, but the doctor credits them with saving my life.

I was taken to the nearby University Hospital. That night when I was brought into the emergency ward, closer to death than life, only one doctor was at the hospital. He was an elderly surgeon who spent most of his time lecturing at the medical college and was reputed to be the finest surgeon in all of Japan. He performed an emergency operation on me, doing the necessary amputations and treating me for shock.

At the time I would have cursed the fate that protected me. I did curse it when I regained consciousness a week later, and many times after that when I learned the full extent of my injuries. But God was continuing to work. I understand many things now that I didn't when I was first taken to the hospital. God had placed those men on the train so they could keep me alive by giving me first aid seconds after my suicide attempt. He brought the famed surgeon to the hospital that night and kept him there so he would be available when the ambulance brought me in.

Why God would bother Himself with such a one as I, I do not know. Many are the times I have asked myself that question without knowing the answer. But now I shall never stop thanking and praising Him for it.

For a week I remained unconscious, waking only enough to realize I was in the hospital. Dimly I knew I was given several blood transfusions and was being fed intravenously. I also became aware of the fact that my left arm was gone and my right hand was heavily bandaged.

At first I didn't know how seriously my hand was injured, and Yuriko, who was at the hospital constantly, helping to take care of me, didn't want to say.

"Your hand is getting better," she would tell me.

"But why is it wrapped like this?" I kept pressing for the reason until she told me reluctantly.

"You still have your thumb and two fingers."

My thumb and two fingers! That meant two fingers were gone. It was not enough that I had to lose an arm. My other hand was mutilated as well. A new agony wrenched my soul.

I don't know why, but my first thoughts were of the things I had been doing so often with my friends. I held out my mutilated hand and stared at it.

"At least I can still go skating," I said aloud.

Yurika choked and turned quickly to slip out of the room as though she was suddenly ill. I was puzzled. What had happened to her?

There was a tent like a canopy over the lower half of the bed; and when the doctor dressed my injuries, he blindfolded me. I didn't know, then, that my legs were gone.

As soon as I was feeling a little better, the chief of police came to see me. He was a kindly man who must have found that particular part of his job most distasteful. He looked as though he was far more interested in trying to help me than in asking questions.

"Aren't you glad you're alive?" he asked as he sat down beside the bed.

My mouth curved bitterly. I thought he was ridiculing me because I had not been successful in taking my life. But he wasn't. He must have been trying to cheer me up, to help me see there was something else to live for. He told me about the two men who were on the train and saved my life.

"You have them to thank for being alive today," he informed me. "Aren't you lucky? Aren't you glad those men were able to help you?"

"Why should I be glad about that?" I demanded angrily. "Why didn't they let me die?"

He could have sent one of his men to get my story for the records, but he came himself. I have never found out why he took such an interest in me. I've often wondered if he hadn't had a firsthand experience with suicide himself. Perhaps a son or daughter of his had been successful in what I attempted, and he wanted to do what he could to keep me from trying again.

But I didn't want their interference. Couldn't they see? There was no reason for living. Death was the only way out! Why did everyone pretend my problems were gone? Why did they act as though life should be appealing once more?

Why couldn't they all have left me alone? A person should have the right to decide whether he wanted to live or not. This was the thesis of some Japanese philosophers on the subject. Why did those people have to interfere and make me do it over again?

Thank them? Why should I thank them? I wanted to curse them to their teeth.

Yuriko seldom left my room, either day or night, and Yasuzo and his wife and Akiyoshi visited me frequently. But my father did not come. I wondered about it, but when I asked the others in the family, they would give me some lame excuse about his not feeling well or being busy at the office. It was weeks before he could bring himself to the hospital to see me, and months before I learned the reason why. I was complaining about it when Yuriko broke her silence.

"We talked it over," she said, irritation tightening her mouth. I knew she was upset. "Yasuzo decided it was better to spare you this, but I can't have you feeling that our father doesn't care. That is the reason he hasn't come to see you. He cares so much he cannot bring himself to see you like—like this." She gestured helplessly.

She went on to tell me how he had paced the floor all night after the police first brought the news of my attempted suicide.

"Why?" he would say aloud. "Why would Yoneko do such a thing? And what can I do to help her? I've tried everything. Everything!"

I felt like crying after that and was terribly ashamed of myself. I thought I knew Father well, but I was beginning to see that I didn't know him at all. He was a strange man, withdrawn and inarticulate, especially after the death of my mother. I suppose some might say he was afraid to face reality. As far as I was concerned, that didn't matter. He loved me!

In the hospital I am sure I was difficult for Yuriko to take care of. Mother had always obeyed my slightest whim, even in what she fixed for me to eat. In the hospital I was arrogant and demanding. I didn't have any appetite, except for certain foods which were usually out of season. For a time all I wanted was mandarin oranges. Then it was watermelon.

I'll never know how my family found watermelon for me in the middle of the winter. We had never had watermelon in late February before. Even now, I am surprised they were able to find it at all. The price they paid for it must have been staggering. But they found a watermelon and brought it to me. I'm not sure I appreciated it half as much as I should have.

I must have been heavily sedated those first few weeks. I slept so much and my mind was so fogged I had difficulty in remembering who came to see me and who didn't. The doctor was beginning to get concerned.

"You must not sleep so much, Yoneko," he would say. "Try to sit up and stay awake."

I would open my eyes and stare hazily at him. "I'm so drowsy," I would mumble. "I can't stay awake."

They would try to raise me up in bed so I wouldn't be so apt to fall asleep, but whenever they did I became dizzy. Everything I looked at went around and around and around. I wanted only to lie still and sleep. I am sure it was my own desire as much as the medication that kept me dozing so much. When I was sleeping, I could not think. Thinking about my arm and my missing fingers—as well as the bungled attempt to end my suffering by taking my life—disturbed me. I still did not know about my legs. That blow was yet to come.

"My toes itch, Yuriko," I would complain.

A look of horror crossed her taut features, and for an instant she seemed as old as our mother had been when she died.

"Scratch them for me."

Helplessly she reached under the canopy on the bed and pretended to scratch toes that were not there.

"Harder. I can't even feel it!"

She annoyed me. There was nothing about scratching toes to bring tears to her eyes.

Finally the time came when they took down the canopy and the doctor told me to sit up in bed. Fear seized Yuriko.

"Do you think she is ready, Doctor?"

Hai," he said curtly. "It is time." He stayed in the room, but I wasn't ready to sit up then and I said so. I still was so independent I resisted doing anything unless I wanted to. He acted as though he was about to order me to sit up, but he changed his mind with the words still on his lips. He shifted his attention to my older sister.

"I will be in the lounge if you need me."

I resented being ignored, and my mangled body stiffened. I was the one who would be sitting up, and I didn't need his help. It wouldn't be long until I would be able to take care of myself without assistance from Yuriko or anyone else, I reasoned. By this time I knew something was amiss. My mouth was hot and dry, and an icy dread began to grow deep in my heart.

When he was gone, I glared at Yuriko and struggled to push myself erect.

"Here, I'll help you."

"I don't need any help," I muttered.

I had made up my mind not even to try anymore, and I fell back on the pillows, breathing heavily. Then I remembered how much trouble I had using a bedpan and how much I hated it. If I could begin to sit on the side of the bed, it wouldn't be long until I would be able to go to the toilet by myself.

After a few moments I tried again. My sister wanted to help me, but I ordered her away. Somehow I managed to scoot myself around on the bed and with my one arm pushed myself erect. A normal person could have caught herself; but when I started forward, I had no means of stopping. I slipped off the side of the bed and was on my knees on the floor.

I cried out in agony and frustration and pain. Now I knew the truth! I not only had lost my arm and two fingers on the other hand, but both legs as well! I was a hopeless, helpless cripple!

I did not move. I did not even try but remained on my knees just as I had fallen and cried inconsolably. My sobbing echoed down the quiet hospital hall. And I didn't care.

The next few minutes were a jumble I have not yet unraveled. Yuriko must have dashed for help. The doctor and a nurse came running to my room and got me back to bed. Then a sedative stopped my crying and began to dull my mind. Mercifully, I slept.

For days after that I lay motionless on the bed, keeping my face to the wall. I refused to talk to anyone, even when they questioned me.

I could never live a normal life. I decided that not even my father and brother would be able to find a husband for me now. And I had resented their efforts a few short weeks ago, I recalled bitterly. Who would want to marry half a woman? I wouldn't be able to shop or clean house or care for children. I would never know the meaning of love for a husband or the joys of a family.

I said nothing to indicate to anyone what was on my mind. I wasn't going to be thwarted again by some well-meaning person who couldn't understand that for some people, living was worse than death.

But the doctor seemed to know my thoughts. His orders were firm. The sash on my kimono-type pajamas was taken away. So were the fruit knives that were brought with my apples and oranges. I was to get no knives of any kind—nothing that could be used to take my life.

I spent most of my waking hours trying to think of some way to accomplish my purpose in spite of the close watch they kept on me. It wasn't long until I thought of a simple plan. I had been in the hospital enough to know the weak spots in their routine and in the people who came in to take care of me. Every night I would complain of pain and sleeplessness.

"Isn't there something you can give me?" I would ask.

The doctor prescribed some sleeping pills to be given at the discretion of the nurses. That was all I needed. Triumphantly, I began to horde them, hiding them under my pillow, under the mattress, in all sorts of places where I thought they would not be apt to find them.

By now Father was coming to visit me. I asked him to move me to a hospital in Hachioji City so I would be closer to home. For some reason I had decided I wanted to die in the city where I had grown up, in the place where Mother had died.

I knew nothing of Jesus Christ, and I had a profound hatred of anything religious, but God used my own fevered irrational reasoning to move a step closer toward bringing me to Himself. Hachioji was where Akitoshi Tahara lived.

SIX

I was saving each new pill with an almost animal cunning, taking pleasure in each addition to my deadly little horde and the fact that I was managing to escape discovery. Moving to a different hospital had not made adding to my ticket to eternity any more difficult. I had only to look sorrowfully up at the doctor and complain of pain and sleeplessness. He was soon having the nurses give me medication for pain whenever I asked for it.

I knew this time I would succeed. A strange exultation took hold of me. Taking my life was all I thought about. As I went to sleep at night I mentally counted my pills and speculated at the number I would have to save before I could be sure I had enough. When I woke up in the morning my first consideration was for my hiding place of the day. I moved them regularly to keep them from being discovered.

I had worked everything out most carefully. It was a grisly game, made even more fascinating by the fact that I was sure of winning. They would not know until it was over how clever I was. I was still as despondent as ever, but knowing I soon would put an end to my miserable existence made the days bearable.

I still cannot remember any word of encouragement brought to me by the doctors. No one mentioned the possibility that I might be able to get artificial limbs. No one explained to me that I could have a normal, happy life. Perhaps it was just as well. I was so disturbed that I doubt that I would have heard anything they might have said to me.

Akitoshi Tahara did not know of my existence at the time, but we were soon to be thrust together. He had been a believer for almost two years and had just dedicated his life to full-time service. The missionaries, who had so much difficulty pronouncing his name correctly that they called him "Andy," considered him an answer to their prayers.

The Fox family was soon to leave on furlough, and the McLeroys, who were to take their place, had already moved to Hachioji. They had been in Japan for some time and had advanced in their study of the language to the place where Robin was able to do some preaching and visitation, but he needed the help of someone who knew both the language and the people.

"God has sent you to us," he would tell Akitoshi. "He is going to use you in a wonderful way."

Akitoshi hoped that was true. At times he wondered.

The four missionaries were continuing their study of the language, but they were dissatisfied with their progress. They decided they could learn more if they had a private tutor come to the house. Akitoshi and Robin McLeroy went to inquire at the high school I had been attending and talked to two of the teachers. The younger was particularly interested and took the job. He was one of the teachers I had gone to in my bewildered search for help.

The first link between Akitoshi and myself was established in another of God's mysterious moves. We were about to be brought together by one who understood something of the Christian faith and what God can do in a life, although he was not a believer himself. The teacher often talked about his family and his work as he visited with Akitoshi and the missionaries.

"Do you ever go to the hospitals and visit?" he asked one morning.

"Often," Robin told him.

"I thought so. My wife is a Catholic, so I know a little of what you Christians believe."

He went on to tell them about me, how I had gone to him repeatedly for help and he had tried as hard as he could, but without success. The next thing he knew I had thrown myself under a train. It was a miracle I had not been killed.

Actually, the teacher asked Robin to call on me, but the American invited Akitoshi, his Japanese friend, to go along. Akitoshi suggested that they buy a package of candy or some fruit for me. In Japan it is customary always to take a gift when you go to the hospital to see someone. He also had a New Testament which he gave to me. I was too shy to say anything to him about it, but I resented the book. I even resented their coming.

Oh, I thought when they told me who they were and what they were doing. *Two of those! Well, it's not going to do you any good.*

I didn't know anything about Christianity, but I hated it as passionately as I hated Tenri-kyo and Buddhism and all religions. And why wouldn't I hate religion? It was religion that had cost my mother's life.

If they had only let me call the doctor the morning she had her second stroke, I thought, *she would still be alive and I wouldn't be lying here helplessly, with everyone pitying me.* I had no way of knowing for sure that the adherents of Tenri-kyo in our neighborhood caused Mother's death by insisting on their holy water and prayers instead of allowing me to call Dr. Yenai, but in my blind, unreasoning hurt I was sure that it was true. *And, if she had lived,* I told myself, *I would never have considered taking my life.* It was easy to understand why I had such resentment against religion. At least it seemed reasonable to me.

I tried to be polite, even though the men were strangers and uninvited. We Japanese take pride in our courtesy and hospitality. I could not have been rude to them, regardless of how I felt.

They are going to try to push that stuff at me, but I am not going to listen, I promised myself, steeling my mind and heart against them. *They'll soon find out they are wasting their time making calls on me.*

Akitoshi kept looking at me strangely. He told me later it was because I was so pretty. He also thought there was something familiar about my face; he was sure he had seen me somewhere. Later, when we got to be friends and talked about it, we decided he must have seen me go by his father's bicycle shop. It was not far from my home.

But I squirmed under his shy gaze. *He's feeling sorry for me,* I fumed inwardly. *Well, he can keep his pity!*

I don't know whether they sensed my displeasure or if they were pressed with other calls, but they didn't stay in my room long. On the way home, Robin told Akitoshi that I had greatly disturbed him. When he first saw me, I looked as though I was the saddest person in all the world. That wasn't far from wrong. I had forgotten what it was like to have a singing heart.

After they left and I was alone, I took the pills from their hiding place and counted them. I wished I knew how many it would take to wipe out my miserable existence. If I could be sure I had enough, I would take them that very night.

But God plagued me with doubt. If I failed this time, I would lose that opportunity. There would be no way open to me to commit suicide before I was released from the hospital. And that might be months.

So I waited.

The following Sunday afternoon they were back again. I was disturbed that they had returned. I thought I had discouraged them enough so that they would stop bothering me. I couldn't understand why any Japanese would constantly associate himself with the hated Americans and their religion and allow them to call him by the ridiculous name of Andy. Well, they would soon learn I was poor material for conversion.

I'm not going to listen to that religious junk of theirs, I again promised myself when I saw them approaching my bed.

I was determined not to show any interest in what they were saying. I refused to talk to them or answer their questions unless they were so pointed I felt I had to. Even then, I mostly answered just "yes" or "no" or shook my head. I scarcely looked at either of them.

I was constantly irritated and miserable. Before the accident I had always acted happy and carefree, even though I was terribly depressed and miserable about my mother's death. Everyone remarked about it. Now I was obviously morose and heavy of heart. Everything was weighed and found wanting by the tragedy that had befallen me.

When I woke up in the morning and saw that it was going to be a bright, cloudless day, resentment would burn within me.

What good will weather like this do for me? I can never go out and enjoy it.

And the birds that were singing were doing it to mock me. They were free and I was a slave to my bed. When Father or my brothers brought me flowers, I had to fight to keep from revealing how much I hated the blossoms. They were beautiful, reminding me of the dresses Mother used to make for me.

How that wrenched at me. I would never have such pretty dresses again. And it would mean nothing if I did. I wouldn't be able to go anywhere.

I longed to have some of my friends come and see me. When some of them did, however, they were embarrassed and didn't know what to say. It seemed so unnatural for them that they had trouble finding something to talk about. But Akitoshi and his American friend never seemed to have any difficulty, and I hadn't even known them until a few days before. The others were friends I had grown up with. I had gone skating and to parties and bars with them. I knew them as well as I knew my family.

Father and Yuriko always seemed embarrassed when I had visitors and they were present. They would snatch up the nearest blanket and tuck it around the lower half of my body as though I was in danger of a sudden chill. I learned later that their concern was not for themselves but for me. They thought it would bother me to have friends come and see my legs. But I was so filled with self-pity that I interpreted their concern as being for themselves.

I'm a terrible disgrace to my family, I reasoned. *They're ashamed of me. That proves they don't love me. I'm giving them so much trouble. It would be better for everyone if I were dead.*

And my thoughts went back to my growing cache of pills. One day there would be enough of them. Then I would no longer cause anyone difficulty.

Akitoshi and his friend continued to come back to see me about once a week, but I wasn't very nice to them. I would not allow them to talk to me, though I did enjoy their singing. They thought they were getting their message through to me, but they really weren't. I liked the melodies but I could not understand the meaning of the words. What did I know of "peace" and "going home" and being "saved by the blood of Jesus Christ"?

When they left, my heart was as stone against them. I was firm in my resolve not to encourage them to come back, yet I found their visits comforting. That, I could not understand. Even though I didn't want them to come, and though I would not allow them to read the Bible or pray with me or talk with me about their God, I was being drawn to Him. It was almost as though I could hear Him calling to me.

And I didn't like it.

There were other things about Akitoshi and his American friend that impressed me, although I would not have admitted it. Most of the people I knew were so polite that promises came easily. And they were as easily forgotten. But not with these men. They actually kept their word. If they said they would come back to see me on a certain day or would bring something for me or would do a favor for me, there was never any question. They did it. It seemed almost stupid the way they were so concerned about doing what they said they would. They were either out of their minds, I reasoned, or were entirely different than anyone I had ever known.

I was furious when I discovered I was actually looking forward to their visits. I was even more determined that they were not going to be successful in involving me in their religion. I had seen religion fail. It was empty and meaningless, a mockery to everyone foolish enough to get involved in it. I didn't realize how well I was getting my opposition across to my visitors.

After a month or so, Akitoshi was sure it was useless for them to continue seeing me. He always has been able to read my moods better than I could read them myself.

"She's not interested in anything we say. It's a waste of time to keep going back."

"Don't get discouraged,' Robin told him. "I have a feeling about that girl."

They talked often about me, weighing the things I had said, trying to read what I meant. Meanwhile, they continued to call on me. Later the American told Akitoshi there were many times when he had to fight against the same conviction that further visits were useless. My heart was too hard and my discouragement was too great to ever yield to Christ, he would reason. How grateful I am that God would not allow their lack of confidence to stop their visits.

The Foxes had a pair of parakeets, and at about the time my callers had become the most discouraged, Margaret decided it would be nice for me to have the birds. Had she followed the strict Japanese custom, they would have brought them to my room and left them. But Robin asked if I wanted them. I completely misinterpreted their motives.

These people are only trying to be nice, I decided. *They want to make a good impression on me, but they can't buy my heart.*

I really wanted those parakeets, but I was sure they would forget all about bringing them. I knew my best friend would volunteer to do something for me but would forget about it.

However, the next time my visitors came, they brought the birds along. That action spoke to me in a way that their words could never have done.

I was not aware of it then, but Akitoshi said they saw a slight change in my attitude after that. I was still hard set against their religion, and most of the time they were well aware of my determination not to have anything to do with their beliefs. Yet, there were days when they thought they could see that I was a little softer, a little more friendly.

Easter came and with it a special speaker to the little church where Akitoshi and his American friends served Christ. An American by the name of Shelton Allen was to preach that Sunday. He could speak Japanese quite well.

He had a message prepared for the evening service, but during the singing that night God began to speak to him about it. Reluctantly, he pushed aside his prepared sermon and began to make notes on the thoughts that came to him. The new message was on Christ's walk to Emmaus with two of His disciples after the resurrection and contained no earth-shaking revelations. Yet, it was exactly what I needed—although at the time he was speaking nobody even supposed I would ever hear it—because it revealed to me the truth that Christ lives.

Akitoshi said Mr. Allen was disturbed at the close of the meeting. There were new faces in the crowd, and in those days an average of one or two persons a Sunday were committing their lives to Christ. There was no response at that meeting, however.

"I can't understand it," Mr. Allen told his friends. "Do you suppose I made a mistake about the message?"

About that time an American GI came up and introduced himself. He was a good friend of Roger and Margaret Fox, having gotten acquainted with them some time before when they were ministering near Tachikawa Air Base, where he was stationed. He had just bought a new American-made tape recorder. It was a huge, cumbersome piece of equipment which he lugged all the way to the church on a crowded train.

"I don't know why I brought this monstrosity down here. I don't even know why I taped the message. I'm not all that sharp on Japanese. I'm lucky if I can understand enough to know what I'm ordering in a cafe. But I'm going to leave the recorder and the tapes with you for awhile. Maybe you can think of some way of using them."

I'm not sure, but I think it was Akitoshi who said, "Why don't we take it and let Yoneko-san listen to it."

Neither of the men expected any response from me. It was just that tape recorders were new and still a novelty that they thought I would enjoy hearing one. And it was one more opportunity of sharing the message of Jesus Christ with me.

They were so busy that week that it was not until Thursday or Friday evening that they had time to come to the hospital to see me. It was nine o'clock in the evening when they arrived, carrying that box that looked half as big as a coffin to me.

God had been preparing me for their visit. I was having one of my bad days, thinking of death and those white tablets that would soon bring me release. When I saw who had come to call on me so late in the evening, my heart groaned.

Oh, no! I exclaimed inwardly. *Not again! Anything but listening to them!* I didn't even want to hear them sing. All I wanted was to be left alone.

I don't remember how I treated them or if they asked me about listening to the tape. All I know for certain is that I was soon caught up in the words of the speaker. He was talking about Christ dying on the cross and coming to life again so I could put my trust in Him.

He didn't care that I had lost both legs and an arm and two fingers on my hand, as far as loving me was concerned. He didn't care about my hatred of Him. He had come to earth to live and had died on the cross and rose again from the grave to save such a one as I! He loved me, Yoneko, so much, that He did all of that just so I could be with Him. And He had come to the two men on the road to Emmaus and walked with them so I could hear about it and know for sure that He had conquered death. I saw that, in spite of all that had happened, He loved me and wanted to bring me to Himself!

I wasn't conscious that the speaker was saying any more than that, or the fact that he was talking to anyone else. It seemed as though he was actually in the room with me, sitting on the chair that held the recorder. And God was using his voice to talk to me.

By the time the speaker was half finished, great tears escaped my tenacious hold on them and rolled down my cheeks. When the message was over and Akitoshi turned off the machine, his solemn eyes pierced the curtain I tried to keep between us.

"Would you like to pray, Yoneko-san?" he asked quietly.

"God help me!" I prayed. I thought I had wiped the tears away, but they still streamed down my cheeks. I was only aware that my eyes were hot. "God help me!" I kept repeating.

As I prayed those three simple words, my thoughts raced. *I am going to put my whole life on this God. Everything. Whatever there is for me in the future belongs to Him.*

Akitoshi and Robin didn't talk much after that. At least I was not aware of it if they did. It seems they packed up the recorder and left in a few minutes. As soon as they were gone, I closed my eyes. The next thing I knew it was seven o'clock the next morning. I was astonished at the simple fact that I had slept through an entire night. It had been months since I had slept so soundly.

I looked around. The sky was blue and cloudless and the May sun was coaxing the flowers to bloom.

It is beautiful this morning, I thought.

That startled me.

Why am I thinking this way? I wondered. For me there had been no beautiful days since that horrible night in Tokyo.

I looked at my watch. Breakfast would not be ready for another hour. I picked up the New Testament they had left on their first visit. I cannot understand how it was still around.

Pondering what had happened the night before, I opened the Testament and began to leaf through it from the back to the front. I had always done that, thinking the best part of any book was at the back. As I did so, I read a few phrases or sentences at random. Most had no meaning for me.

Yet, God was working. He had to show me what He had done for me. I was still bewildered by it. A few minutes later one short phrase leaped out at me.

*"If any man be in Christ, he is a new creature."**

*2 Corinthians 5:17.

I almost shouted, I was so excited. This was it! This was what had happened to me!

There was an older woman in her mid-fifties sharing the room with me. Although she was still asleep, I was so thrilled with the change in my life that I had to tell someone! I woke her up and explained to her what a marvelous thing Christ had done for me.

"If it is as wonderful as you say it is," she told me, "I'll be interested in knowing more about it."

I could scarcely wait for Akitoshi and his friend to come back so I could tell them God had finally answered their prayers. Everything about me had changed.

SEVEN

Spring had come. From my hospital window I could see no clouds in the vast blue sky, and the visible wedge of houses and trees and little yards was washed with a bright, warm sun. Flowers had been awakened gently and teased into blooming, and the children, who seemed to have sprung from the ground along with the flowers, were everywhere, finding new joy just in being alive.

And so was I.

Spring had come to my heart the past few days. The long, bleak winter of despair was gone, banished from my life. The deadly sleeping tablets I had been hoarding were forgotten in my pillowcase. Now that I was a believer in Jesus Christ I was a new person. I could laugh and look forward to each new day with anticipation and happiness.

My family could not understand it. One afternoon I was dull and empty, a withered husk of the girl I had been before my mother died. I was wrung dry and looking only to the release death would bring. I had not mentioned suicide to them in weeks and they did not mention it to me, but they knew what I was planning and felt powerless to stop it. When they left my room the fear of it was written in their eyes.

Returning the next evening, they were astonished by what they found. The recent sad Yoneko was gone. The former Yoneko of more delightful days had taken her place. I could smile again without bitterness, and a new peace gleamed in my eyes. After months of thinking only of myself, as though there was no one else who had ever faced heartache and disappointment, I was concerned about Father and Yuriko and my two brothers. I wanted to know what they were doing and if they were well. I asked about Yasuzo's wife and how school was going for Akiyoshi.

They were as perplexed by this new mood as they were pleased by it. It was a relief to have me more like myself. Still, they wondered. At home there was much talking about the change that had come over me. They tried to figure out what had happened and if it would last.

"Perhaps she is excited and gay because she has worked out some way to take her life," Father said. So much sadness had come to him since Mother's first illness that he could not believe this was anything more than the first portent of another blow. "I have heard this sometimes happens to those who are planning to kill themselves," he continued.

I tried to explain to them how Jesus Christ had forgiven me and had taken over my life. I tried to make them see that He was the One who had taken away the heaviness from my soul and given me peace and the courage to go on living.

They did not understand.

I suppose they did not try very hard. Like my teachers advised me to do with spiritual problems that were difficult to understand—like the meaning of life and death—they pushed them aside. This was the doing of the fanatical young Akitoshi Tahara and his American friends, they decided. It would not last. After I was home with them for awhile I would see the folly of such foolish ideas.

I was just like our mother, a fine woman of strong will and character, but emotional when it came to religion. With Mother it was Tenri-kyo. With me it was this Christ who filled my life. Each carried a different set of superstitions involving different gods, they decided, but the results were the same, an almost childish fanaticism.

However, they were thankful something had come along to distract me from myself and my troubles. Perhaps this break in my black mood would be permanent. Perhaps I would have the strength to go on living with some degree of happiness after I became disillusioned with my new religion, as they were sure I would. They only hoped that the disillusionment would come slowly, a precept at a time, so it would not be such a shock to me.

But they reckoned only on human strength and frailties. They reckoned without our God. I had a new purpose to life—new direction and strength. God was giving me a peace I had never known before, even as a child. I trusted Him even more completely than I trusted my mother when I put my chubby little hand in hers and we walked confidently across a busy street.

I was still a child when it came to understanding God and His Word. There was so little I knew about Him. Akitoshi and the missionaries were concerned about me. They knew, even better than I realized, how antagonistic my family was to my new faith in Christ. They knew how hard it would be for me to continually face the arguments of my college student brothers. When I was released from the hospital several weeks after making my decision for Christ, Margaret Fox volunteered to have Bible study with me every week and Akitoshi came along to interpret. Those Bible studies had much to do with helping me to live a Christian life at home.

I longed to share Christ with my family, but it was all but impossible for me to say anything to Father or my brothers. I found it easier to talk with Yuriko about Jesus Christ. There was a closeness between us, born when our mother died. We needed each other.

There were five years separating our ages. There were days when those years seemed but a month or two and we were more like (how do you say it?) *futagos.** On other days we were an entire generation apart. Yuriko became almost like a mother to me and I could talk with her about anything. When I spoke so haltingly of receiving Christ, she listened intently and I was beginning to believe she was becoming interested in my Saviour. Then she laughed at me.

"You sound as though you are in love with this Jesus," she taunted.

I was so anxious to let her know what Christ had done for me, I did not even notice the scorn in her voice. "I do love Him. He has given me such peace and joy that I can't thank Him enough. And He can do the same for you."

Her smile was indulgent, as though I were her five-year-old daughter and had fastened my affection on some foolish object I would soon tire of. "You'll change," she said confidently. "This religion that has you in such a glow will get drab and dull as soon as you've had time to think about it. It won't be long until you'll be back with us in what you believe. This will pass."

"I wouldn't even want to live without Jesus Christ," I told her.

Her scornful laughter penetrated the paper partitions that separated one room from another. "It won't last, Yoneko," she said. "If you're a Christian in fifteen years, come back and talk to me again. Then I'll be one, too."

Our brother Akiyoshi, who was in another part of the house, heard Yuriko's laughter and came out to see what was going on.

"Yoneko is trying to get me on my knees before this God of hers," she told him.

"Watch what you're about!" he exploded angrily. "One idiot in the family is enough!"

*Twins.

Most of the time Yuriko was patient and kind with me, but there were days when her bitterness was apparent, like the souring of milk. Father said nothing about it, but both my sister and I knew that he still refused to give her permission to marry because of me. He talked of building a house for me and fixing things so I could live alone, but months passed and nothing was done. Looking back, I think he was waiting for an indication that I would be able to take care of myself.

I was as disturbed as Yuriko and could not blame her for being unhappy. Yet, I was caught in the same trap. On occasion the tension between us mounted.

"Why do I have to do all the work?" she complained.

"I do what I can," I replied. I have to admit now that that was not entirely true. I was only eighteen and not above taking advantage of my situation if it seemed expedient.

She pushed a loose strand of hair from her eyes. "You don't really mean that."

"But I do. And there are other things I could do, if you would only tell me what you want me to take care of."

"You could clean the butsudan."

She saw the horror on my face as she mentioned the family shrine or altar of the Buddhas.

"What's the matter now?" she demanded irritably.

I was sure she had asked me to clean the butsudan out of contempt for my faith in Jesus Christ. Thinking back, I'm sure that is being unfair to her. She knew so little about what it meant to be a Christian that she could not have known how I would feel about doing that. With a prayer for help, I explained.

"That is one thing I can't do," I said. I was more miserable than I had been since coming home from the hospital. I had to do something to help Yuriko. She had every right to expect it. She carried the load of shopping for food and cleaning the house and waiting on me. I *had* to do what I could to help her. Only this thing she asked me to do was against everything my new faith in Jesus Christ stood for.

"It isn't difficult."

"I know." By this time I was able to get around the house quite well on my stumps. "It's just that I am a Christian now and—and I can't work with the god shelf."

Anger flecked her eyes as she wheeled away.

"Wait, Yuriko!" I cried impulsively. "If you'll clean the butsudan I'll clean the kitchen or the bathroom or do the dirtiest job in the whole house—the one you hate doing more than anything else."

When she saw I was sincere, there was a perceptible change in her manner.

"You can clean the bathroom," she said. "I hate cleaning the toilet bowl worse than anything else."

From then on I took care of the bathroom and she cleaned the family shrine. After that incident we were closer to each other than ever. Once in a while she would tease me about my faith, but this never happened in front of anyone else. There were other times when she chafed at the fact that I stood in the way of her marriage, and she was bitter and complaining. I was more conscious of her problems, however, and tried harder than before to do my share of the work.

After that terrible encounter with my family on the night when they demanded that I forsake Christ and Akiyoshi slapped me, my brother's bitterness against my Christian friends frequently controlled his tongue. But I scarcely heard him. I knew what he was saying about Akiyoshi and the Foxes was not true. Besides, even if they did stop being my friends, it wouldn't matter. I had Jesus.

As I began to learn more about God, I longed to share my faith with others. I wanted to help in the way that Akitoshi Tahara and Margaret and Roger Fox and the McLeroys were helping. I knew I could not do many of the things the others did. I couldn't preach or go from door to door. I thought I could teach Sunday school, and I hoped God would be able to use me in other ways—ways I could not yet understand.

I was reading my Bible one day when God gave me a special verse. I had heard the others talk about that happening. I wondered how they could know it was a verse just for them. I also wondered whether I would be able to recognize it if God intended a verse for me. I used to pray I wouldn't miss it if God had a verse He wanted to use to speak to my heart. I don't know for sure what I expected, or if I expected any particular way He would use to make it known to me. I need not have been concerned. The verse reached out and grabbed me.

"This is for you, Yoneko!" I realized.

I read it again, tingling with excitement. "I will do a new thing. I will show you a new thing that is hidden from anybody."† I am probably not quoting it correctly, but that is the meaning of the words.

What joy seized my soul! God did have something special for me! He was going to use me. A new strength surged through my body. I could not praise Him enough. I would not be spending a life of idleness. My God had a job for me to do.

There was a change in my Sunday school class I was teaching that I had not anticipated. God was blessing my efforts in a new way. I was completely surrounded by children and happier than I had ever been.

The little church we went to was having special meetings at the close of the year, and everyone was praying for their success. I was closely involved in the planning and the praying, but there were some prayers I was not told about. Akitoshi and his friends were praying I would dedicate my life for the Lord's service. They said nothing to me about it because they

†See Isaiah 43:19.

didn't want me to make such a decision because I thought they wanted it. The call had to come from God.

On New Year's Eve there was a service in the Foxes' home. I had not mentioned it to anyone, but God had been dealing with me. While I was praying prior to that very meeting, I dedicated my life to Christ and His service. I was the first to speak during the testimony portion of the service.

"I must tell you what has just happened to me," I said. "I have told the Lord I would give myself to Him completely. If He is willing, I am going to Bible school to learn more about the Bible."

I didn't know how I could get the money. I didn't even know whether my father would let me go, but I was positive I had to. The fact that Akitoshi was in his second year at the same school did not influence me.

I liked him as a friend. I thought he must be one of the smartest persons I had ever met. When he was interpreting for Margaret Fox, he often answered the questions himself rather than referring them to her. Still, I did not once think about marrying him. He was too far above me for that. I knew my own weaknesses and how little I understood of the Bible. A man like Akitoshi would never be interested in someone like me.

My father was not a Christian, but he was a good man and loved me deeply. When I talked with him about Bible school, he surprised me by saying he would pay my expenses.

"You know I do not approve of this religion of yours, Yoneko," he said to me.

I waited, steeling myself against the attack I was sure would come.

"But I am glad you have something you can devote your life to and work for. I am glad it makes you happy."

Even though I had never once considered the fact that Akitoshi might be interested in marrying me, I enjoyed being with him. For that reason I was pleased that I would be going to the same school. I would have at least one friend among all those students.

I don't know when I began to realize he was in love with me. It came slowly, in a score of different ways. The first time he sat beside me, I scarcely noticed. When it continued to happen, however, I saw that it was more than coincidence. And he was continually doing thoughtful little things for me. He adjusted my pillows and once in awhile would bring me some flowers he knew I liked.

I didn't believe I cared for him any more than as a friend but I was disturbed when I learned he was having some problems with hemorrhoids during his first year of Bible school. I made him a big, soft cushion with his initials embroidered on it. Another time I made him a new necktie. But I only did those things because he had done so much for me, I reminded myself.

I wasn't going to marry him. I shouldn't marry anybody. Yet, I was thinking of him most of the time. If I ate a piece of candy, I would think, *Akitoshi would like this.* If I got a new understanding of a passage of Scripture, I would wonder if he knew all that it meant. If I saw a sunset that was particularly beautiful or a painting that warmed my heart, I would want to share them with him. But that was as far as my interest was going. Marriage was one thing denied me. I was not concerned about it. At the time I dedicated my life to Jesus Christ and His service, marriage was one area of my future that went on the altar, along with everything else I was or hoped to be.

I don't know who first thought of getting artificial legs for me. The thought had never occurred to me, and Akitoshi told me it had never occurred to him, either. I rather imagine it was the McLeroys or the Foxes. They were concerned about both Akitoshi and me. Roger Fox asked the chaplains and the Christians he met while working with American servicemen to pray for me. It was through them he learned of a famous military surgeon who would be visiting Tokyo on a "round the world" tour of duty. He was an amputee specialist who would be working briefly at the Seventh-Day Adventist Hospital in Tokyo. The Foxes decided he had to see me.

The doctor decided differently, however. His primary responsibility was to American servicemen. He did not see how he could accept all the war-related cases they had arranged for him.

"I wouldn't even be able to crowd an American civilian into my schedule here," he told them. "And this girl is Japanese."

They were unwilling to accept his refusal. Continuing to pray, they aproached him again. Finally, in exasperation, he agreed to look at me. That was all. I would have to have further surgery to prepare the stumps for taking artificial limbs, he said, but he could not promise to do the operations. He would only agree to examine me.

"In fact," he grumbled, "I don't even know why I'm seeing her. I don't have time, you know."

They could have told him his decision had been countermanded by orders from his Superior, but they did not.

I knew nothing about all of this until the day came for me to go to the hospital for my appointment. Roger and Margaret knew it would be difficult to get the overworked surgeon to agree to see me. They didn't want me to start planning on being fitted with artificial legs until they knew whether he would accept me as a patient.

When I went into the little examination room with Margaret, he strode in and closed the door with the brusque attitude of one who was going to get through an unpleasant task as quickly as possible. He sat down at the desk and looked at the stump of my left arm.

"Who did this?" he demanded.

Margaret told him.

He studied it more closely.

"Beautiful," he murmured. "The surgeon who performed this amputation did a beautiful job. I want a picture of this stump."

He examined my legs. They, too, were skillfully done.

"Of course that heel will have to come off. There is no way an artificial limb could be fitted to it. And we will have to do some work on the other stump." He paused. "You won't have to pay me for the surgery. Just make arrangements with the hospital for their bill."

Again God had intervened for me, providing the skill of one of the most famed surgeons the world had seen. I can never understand why He would love me so much.

Akitoshi was baby-sitting for the Foxes the day the call came from the hospital.

"Andy," Margaret had said, "we've got to remember to keep praying for Yoneko-san. She will have to go to the hospital soon and she'll have to have the money to pay her hospital bill. Roger and I decided we ought to ask everybody in the church to pray for her."

It wasn't long after they left the house that the call came from the hospital.

Yes, Akitoshi told the man from the business office who called, he knew about Yoneko-san and that she was scheduled for surgery. He would see that she was there at the appointed time. Yes, he knew she would have to have money enough to pay the bill before the hospital would admit her.

"Do you have the money?" the man asked.

"*Hai,*" Akitoshi retorted quickly. "We have the money."

When he returned the phone to its cradle, he was shaking. He didn't know why he had told the hospital the money was available. He told me he was so anxious to have me get artificial limbs he would likely have promised anything. Margaret was deeply disturbed when she learned what he had done.

"You told the man from the hospital a lie, Andy," she scolded. "Yoneko doesn't have that much money and there's no way we can get it. You ought to know that."

His faith was young and unwavering. His simple trust in the power of God knew no limitations. Anything less than saying we had the money for my stay in the hospital would have been a shocking admission of doubt.

If anyone was at fault for what Akitoshi did, it was I. His feeling for me was so great, and his belief in the power of God was so strong that he couldn't see me getting around the way I did when it was possible for me to have legs I could walk on. I don't know whether he actually had lied as the missionary's wife said, or if he was merely expressing his own confidence that God would supply my need. Although he was stricken by the sharpness of her criticism, he feels now that God prompted him to tell the hospital we had the money. We were trusting God for it, and He did provide.

At the church on Sunday one of the missionaries presented my need. Before we left the sparsely furnished little building, enough money had been pledged to pay for my stay in the hospital. Now only Father's permission stood between me and the operation that would prepare me to be fitted with artificial limbs.

Father was not sure he wanted to give permission for the operation. And he didn't like the thought of taking money from others to pay a bill for someone in his family. He didn't know whether he could stand having me go through surgery again. I was getting along all right the way I was, he reasoned. Wouldn't it be better to leave things as they were? Why should I be asked to suffer again? I had gone through far too much already.

My second brother, Akiyoshi, was furious.

"They must have a reason for begging for money to pay Yoneko's hospital bill!" he blustered roughly. "They've got their own reasons for wanting to be nice to Yoneko. It's shame for you, *Otosan,* and for our entire family! It is best to forget this foolishness!"

My father was of the same opinion about refusing to allow another operation, but for a different reason. "I trust them, Akiyoshi," he said. "And especially the young Japanese man, Akitoshi Tahara. He is an honorable person. He is polite and kind, a credit to his parents."

"He is with *them!"* Akiyoshi spat out the words venomously. "He is the same as they are. They want to use our sister to make gain for themselves."

"We have much to thank them for," Father said quietly. "Yoneko's spirit was dead before they started coming to see her. Now the smile is back on her lips, and the lights dance merrily in her eyes. It means much to me to see her as she now is."

"Bah! You are as taken in as Yoneko! Wait and see! They have something they are keeping from us. And it is for themselves, not for Yoneko. I say, tell them we don't need their filthy yen!"

Father stood, thrusting his hands deeply into his pockets. "I could pay for the hospital myself."

"We don't need their money," Akiyoshi snarled. "Or their operation, either!"

Although Father agreed that the operation was not wanted, he yielded to my plea and gave his consent. And, because I asked him to, he allowed the people in the church to pay for it. Akiyoshi has never been able to understand that, even yet.

For a respectable Japanese family to accept the charity of the hated Christians was unheard of. It was an ugly blot on our family name. But my father granted his permission. There was nothing my brother could do.

Although Father had agreed reluctantly to the operation, it was becoming apparent that Akiyoshi's constant pressure was having its effect. There was going to be no more help from my family as long as I persisted in walking with Christ and associating with my Christian friends. It was soon obvious my family would not be responsible for any of my needs beyond clothing, food, and a place to stay.

Akitoshi learned that the government provided some financial aid for the disabled, and Robin McLeroy went with him to learn more about it. While they were standing in line, Akitoshi turned to his missionary friend.

"Do you think she would be able to get married, Robin?" he asked suddenly.

The missionary knew exactly what he was thinking, although he himself was not aware of it. Robin considered the matter briefly. He and his wife had talked about it a number of times and always came up with the same answer.

"Yes," he said, "I think she could. It would have to be to somebody who would be very kind and understanding, but it would be very possible for her to get married. In fact, I think she would make a good wife for some fine young Christian man."

I knew Akitoshi loved me, although never once did he put words to the deep feelings of his heart. Long before he asked me to marry him, I knew. Don't ask how. I couldn't tell you. Yet I knew exactly how he felt about me. I had also been wrestling with the matter of marriage and coming to the opposite conclusion. Finally, when I was in the hospital for the amputation, he expressed his feelings. Margaret Fox pressured him to talk to me.

"I'm going to write her a letter," he said.

From then on she questioned him about it every time he came around.

"Have you told her, Andy?" she would ask. "Have you written her?"

Finally he talked to me.

"There is something I would like to share with you, Yoneko," he said, "but I wouldn't dare talk to you about it now."

I was surprised by my answer. "I know," I replied. "I feel the same way."

We decided just to keep on praying. We were both going to ask God to talk to us through His Word. Two days later He gave each of us a verse. Akitoshi wrote his on a slip of paper and put it in an envelope. The next time he came to the hospital he gave it to me. I was shaken when I read it. God had given each of us the same verse. How does it go?

"If two of you shall agree on earth as touching any thing that they shall ask, it shall be done for them of my Father which is in heaven."‡

I should have been pleased that the Lord was leading us. Instead, I was greatly annoyed by it. I had been wrestling with the question and had already reached my decision. Foolishly, I made up my mind without seeing God's guidance. When Akitoshi began to talk of marriage, my answers were quick and incisive.

"I don't know how I can be your wife," I told him. "There are so many things I would not be able to do. Being a wife and a mother is a hard lifetime job for anyone with a complete body. I just cannot see how it would work. No, it would not be possible."

He tried to encourage me by relating the story of Abraham and Sarah. They were both so old they were sure it would be impossible for them to have a child, yet God promised

‡Matthew 18:19.

them a son. Even though Sarah was far beyond the age of child-bearing, she conceived and gave birth to Isaac, as God said she would.

"We worship the same God, Yoneko," he reminded me gently. "He can do the same for us."

When I was with him I would begin to think as he did. Later, when I was alone, I would get so discouraged that I was sure marriage was never to be a part of my life. And when we would meet again I would tell him so.

"OK," he would answer, "if you feel that way, I will wait. But we can't change God's mind. You should know that, Yoneko. I'm convinced that He would have us live our lives together. So, I will wait."

He made me angry when he talked that way, because I knew my resolve was weakening. He waited and the time came when I realized he was right. God was leading us together.

I shall never forget the night we went to my father and Akitoshi told him of our plans for marriage and asked for his blessing. My father looked at me strangely, tears leaping to his eyes.

I could not believe it. My father was crying! I had never seen him cry before, not even at my mother's funeral.

"Hai," he said brokenly. "That is good. That is very good. Just take good care of her."

I think I cried, too.

We have never talked with him about that night. It would only increase his shame. As for me, those tears meant much. They were the tears of love.

EIGHT

I was quite young at the time of the war, but I heard my parents talk enough about it to know those years were black for all of us. Those first months of war for Japan seemed to be going exactly as we had been told they would, and everyone looked forward to a bright new day of peace and unsurpassed prosperity.

It was heady news to realize our air force had stunned America by destroying her mighty fleet at Pearl Harbor and our glorious armies leapfrogged their way to the Philippines with little opposition. And when they continued down the string of South Pacific islands toward Australia, we looked confidently for the end of the war.

But our enemies were not crushed. They were only wounded. And we were asked to make sacrifice after sacrifice to slake the ravishing thirst of our war machine. There was no gas for cars. Food was scarce, except for those who were enterprising enough to raise a little garden to bolster their austere rations, and the casualty lists began to mount.

Then the bombs came. They were dropped on our tight little islands infrequently at first, like the scattered raindrops heralding a savage storm. Even Tokyo was visited by those great birds of death. It was a shattering experience, and despair gripped our hearts.

Akitoshi Tahara's father had a small store in Tokyo where he sold medicinal herbs, and for a time the entire family lived there. As the war moved steadily closer to our shores, it was obvious that Tokyo was a major target. Almost every day the B-29s came over, and the exodus from Tokyo and other major cities became a flood. Many moved voluntarily, seeking places in the country or small towns where the bombs were less apt to fall. Others were evacuated by the military. They were forced to leave so that their homes could be knocked down and the streets made wider for the rapid movement of men and equipment in case of the fires that inevitably followed the bombings.

Although Akitoshi's father still maintained his business on the first floor of the house where they lived in Tokyo, he bought a place in Hachioji, the same city where I was raised. God was working in our lives but we were not aware of it then.

Life was becoming increasingly difficult, Akitoshi remembers. A simple task like moving was a major project. It was impossible to get a truck to transport their belongings. And even if they had been able to find one, there was no gas available. So his father hired a man who was fortunate enough to own both a bicycle and a cart. With that frail rig, they were able to transfer their belongings to the house in Hachioji. Nobody remembers how many trips or how many days it took to haul their household goods and clothes fifty miles or more out of the city.

The Taharas dug a shelter in an open place near their new home. Everybody had them, for there was no doubt now that the horror of war would be visited upon us in a very personal way. It was only a matter of when the strikes would come.

Akitoshi's father often remained in the little shop in Tokyo rather than travel home by train. The night of the big bombing, however, he was in Hachioji.

An endless stream of those terrible bombers rained fire and destruction on Tokyo, wiping out hundreds and thousands of homes and crippling that vast city for a time. The sky flamed red and bright as the rising sun, and the thundering explosions shook the earth and threatened to shatter everyone's hearing. The Tahara family huddled in their shelter, certain the end had come and that the next bomb would destroy them.

The older Tahara, like my father, was not particularly religious, in spite of the fact that there was a Shinto shrine in their house in Tokyo. It occupied a prominent place on the main floor where customers would be sure to see it. It was considered good for business to give the appearance of piety. Whenever there was a religious festival, he was one of the first to cooperate by giving his time and money. It really meant little to him personally, except for what it could do in a financial way. The night of the bombing, the gods didn't do much to protect the building, but the family wasn't aware of their loss yet.

Morning light chased the great machines of destruction away, but smoke still hung over the city and fires still raged unchecked. Everyone knew the planes would be back.

"I am going to Tokyo," Akitoshi's father said that morning. "I want to see what it's like. Maybe we have been spared."

Later in the day he returned.

"Everything is gone except my helmet and the safe," he told his family, laughing. "When I came up the street all I could see of our place was the safe with my helmet on top. They stood all alone, as though they were in the middle of a field."

The loss was not as great for him as it was for many. His business had been successful and he was quite wealthy. There was no chance of reestablishing his little shop at the time, but that proved to be no problem.

In August of 1945 the war ended. Nine months later, Akitoshi's mother died quite suddenly. He loved her as much as any son loves his mother, but there were no tears. All his heartache and pain were tightly bottled inside.

Two days later they received word that his brother, who was ten years older than he, had been killed in China.

"We were so far apart in age," he told me, "that we were never like most brothers, but every day I used to stop by the shrine in our neighborhood that honored an old Samurai warrior and pray for his safety. It seems strange now, asking a god I didn't know to keep my brother safe, but I was nothing in religion."

He was thankful his mother did not get word of her oldest son's death before her own. At least she was spared that blow. Hers had not been a happy life like that of my mother. Plagued with a heart condition, her activities were severely limited, and she was burdened with an alcoholic husband.

Akitoshi's father was one of those men who did no drinking at all until he was told by the doctor who was treating him for a threatening stomach ulcer to begin using a little wine.

"Take some wine before you eat," the physician told him. "Then you won't be so hungry and eat so much."

Tahara-san tried to follow the doctor's orders, but a little wine didn't satisfy the newly kindled craving. He was soon taking more and more until he was drinking two quarts a night and became one of the best customers at the neighborhood bar. He was drunk almost every night, a fact that made life difficult for his family.

In the final months of the war and immediately afterward, Akitoshi's father managed to rent a little piece of land which he planted with soy beans and sweet potatoes. It was small, but it did provide them with a little food.

"Like everyone else," Akitoshi told me, "we ate everything available—the leaves and stems of the sweet potato vines, wild greens, nuts, and anything else we could find. Some people had to ride hours on the train just to buy a sack of sweet potatoes and a few beans."

As soon as Tahara-san could, he opened a bicycle shop. By

this time most of their money was gone. Akitoshi worked on the bicycles. His father kept the books. And they lived in the house that was built on the back of the store.

When a friend died, Akitoshi's father married his widow, a woman who had never had a son. She was a stepmother in name but a mother in heart to the bewildered young man. And, as an added benefit, there were three of them to work in the bicycle shop.

Conditions were beginning to improve and Akitoshi should have been happy, but he was not. As far as he could see, there was no honor anymore. Everybody was scrambling to get enough money for food and clothing. Farmers charged as much for their produce as they could get. Never mind that people were hungry. If they didn't have money to pay the price, someone would come along who did. Businessmen juggled their prices at will, charging for extras they didn't give and shortchanging the careless or unwary. No one he knew was honest. Everyone tried to cheat everyone else. Even his own father tried to talk him into deceiving those who traded with them.

"When someone like that fellow comes in, Akitoshi," he said, indicating a customer who appeared to be more gullible than the average, "raise the price. He'll never know the difference."

"But I had already told him what it would cost to put on a new bicycle chain."

"You could have charged him for new parts in the brake."

"I didn't touch the brake."

"Idiot!" His father was growing angry. "He wouldn't know that! How many times do I have to tell you? You'll never make a businessman!"

Their arguments were frequent and bitter, made worse by his father's continual drinking.

Akitoshi was crushed by what he saw and by what his

father incessantly pushed him to do. Even though he had no reason, like religion, to be honest, Akitoshi could not do it. He had to be honest.

A terrible discouragement gripped him. Life had no purpose. It offered only a bleak, meaningless existence, an empty void. In his way, he was as despondent as I had been. He was determined not to do what his father insisted. Surely there was more to life than trampling over one another like so many animals, he reasoned. Yet, he had no answers for his father or himself. There was no one he knew who could give him any hope for the future.

He didn't know why he thought the Christian Church might be able to help him. He knew nothing about it or what it taught. I doubt that he even knew anyone who professed to follow Christ. Still, his desperation was so great that he was ready to try anything. And there was a small Japanese church near his home.

Even visiting the church required more courage than he thought he had. In the eyes of most of the people, the Church of Christ was a tool of the hated Americans, a reminder of the horrible destruction that had fallen upon them. But he went.

He was disappointed in what he heard that first Sunday. The pastor didn't seem to have any more answers to his problems than he did, but he announced that the church would be open every morning for those who wanted to come for a time of prayer.

"I really didn't know what I was hearing," Akitoshi related to me, "or what I was saying when I prayed, but I figured that at least I was doing something."

After a few weeks the pastor informed him that he was now quite zealous and prayerful and was ready for baptism. When that happened he would become a member of the church and there were certain duties and responsibilities that would be his, like coming to the services and giving a certain offering every month.

He didn't know what he should believe, but he knew he wasn't ready for church membership. Besides, the talk of offerings made him wonder if the pastor wasn't like everyone else. It seemed that he, too, was trying to use him to get more money for himself. He quit going to church, and that deep disillusionment and despair once more gripped him.

God had begun to reach out to Akitoshi and He was not willing to let him go so easily. Roger and Margaret Fox drove by occasionally in their beat-up old jeep with the inscription, JESUS SAVES, painted in Japanese on the hood just below the windshield. The words were intriguing, and whenever Akitoshi saw the Americans, a fierce longing took hold of him. He felt that he had to talk to them. But he was shy and they were the enemy of a few short months before. He could never bring himself to approach them.

Because he refused to go to them, God brought them to him. They came into the shop one afternoon looking for a used bicycle. He was so excited that he found it difficult to say anything. They could tell him what the sign on their vehicle meant. Perhaps they could tell him what it was that caused his discouragement. He only hoped that he would have the courage to ask them.

Like practically every other young person in Japan, he was determined to learn English and was in a conversational English club. Unfortunately, all the members of the class were Japanese, and even the instructor was uncertain about some of the pronunciation and the use of certain words.

"We should have someone here to tell us if we are right," he informed the class.

This was Akitoshi's opportunity. "I know an American missionary," he said. "I might be able to get him and his wife to come and help us."

The teacher doubted that they would be interested, but told him to give it a try.

The Americans didn't realize there was such a deep longing in his heart and thought that he only wanted to get their help with the language. As gently as possible, they told him they had come to tell people about Jesus Christ. That was their business. They didn't actually turn him down, but it was obvious they were not too anxious to take the teaching position. However, they did have some questions for him.

"Are you a Christian?" Roger Fox wanted to know.

He couldn't say he was and he couldn't say he wasn't. Then the missionary wanted to know what he thought made a person a believer.

"Being kind," Akitoshi replied, "and reading the Bible and praying every day."

Roger opened the Bible to different Scripture verses and read them aloud. They explained that everyone was a sinner and deserved to die but Jesus Christ brought eternal life.

Akitoshi didn't become a believer that night, but he did join a Bible study that met Wednesday and Thursday evenings. Finally, on September 4, 1952, when he was nineteen, he trusted Christ for his salvation.

His growth as a child of God was slow, however. Everything was so new to him that months passed before he was able to notice any difference in his life.

About the same time his father was getting restless. He had been in the restaurant business before and thought it would be wise to go into it again. He decided to close the bicycle shop and open a little cafe in another part of town.

"You can go with us or not, Akitoshi," he told his son. "The decision is yours."

For some time he had sensed that his son was dissatisfied with the bicycle business, not realizing it was his own dishonesty that disturbed the sensitive Akitoshi. He suggested that he might want to go on to college or get into an entirely different kind of store.

"Maybe you would like to be a merchant better than repairing bicycles."

At the same time, the Foxes were trying hard to get Akitoshi to see that he needed to completely dedicate his life to God. They answered his questions and encouraged him by having him give his own testimony or lead a study of one of the books of the Bible. Occasionally they even asked him to preach. And, whenever the opportunity presented itself, they talked with him about dedicating his life to Christ.

"You will be going to Bible school, won't you?" Roger would ask.

"I can't do that." He was irritated by their persistence. It was almost as annoying as his father's urging him to be dishonest. "I don't have any money and it costs to go to Bible school."

"God will provide for that," they told him.

Such an answer made him furious. God might provide in the States, he countered inwardly, but this was Japan. It was different here.

Thinking to encourage him, they told him of times when they were going to Bible school and how God had given them exactly the amount of money they had to have at precisely the right time. They would get a letter in the mail with money or someone would hand them a check to meet a need that was pressing.

He agreed that such talk sounded nice, but one had to be practical. They had all sorts of Christian friends in the States who were concerned about them. He didn't know anyone except Roger and Margaret Fox who cared that he got to Bible school. Even God wouldn't be able to work in Japan the way He did in America, Akitoshi reasoned. What he was really trying to make himself believe was that God lacked the power to provide for him in the way He had provided for his American friends.

There was another reason he didn't want to follow God's leading. He had made plans for his life and they didn't include Bible school. When he finished the typing courses he was taking, he was going to get a good job and carve out a comfortable life for himself. He didn't want any interference from anyone. But God and the Foxes wouldn't let him rest. He fought savagely against them.

He even went back to the pastor of the church where he first sought help, a man he had grown up with.

"He didn't preach the Bible the way we believe," he confided to me. "I hoped he would say, 'Those missionaries only come to fool you. Follow your choice. Go your own way.' But he didn't. In fact, nobody told me that, and I was getting more and more miserable."

For two or three months he found himself under such strain that he could think of little else. Finally one night he was praying when he realized he had to talk to someone. He went to the Fox home, but they had company. He couldn't interrupt them. Another missionary couple was living a couple of hundred yards away at the time, but he could hear people talking and laughing in their kitchen as he approached. He didn't dare burst into their home with his questions, either.

Bewildered, he wheeled and stumbled down the hill. The road he followed dipped into the valley and twisted upward, clinging to the lip of a sheer cliff. He passed the baseball grounds and climbed upward until he reached a place where he could see the lights of half the city stretching out in a scintillating semicircle.

The matter had to be resolved, and there was no one to help him. No one except God. And he wasn't so sure he wanted God's help right then. He was afraid of what he might be led to do. After all, he had been resisting Him for weeks.

But he had to get things settled. He couldn't go on in the state of agony and confusion that tormented him so sorely.

As he stood there, his heart quieting, God began to speak.

"Look what I have done for you, Akitoshi," He seemed to say. "I have forgiven your sin and saved your soul. I have given you a new life. And how are you repaying Me? By wanting to live selfishly, without considering what I want you to do? Why are you running away from Me?

"I would use you to be a blessing to many people, but you are unwilling. All you have ever wanted to do is run from My leading. There are hundreds of thousands of people right here in this city who do not know I sent My Son to save them. How many believers are there to tell them?

"That is what I am trying to do with your life, Akitoshi. That is what I will do with you if you will only quit fighting Me and allow Me to work My will through you."

That was all it took. He broke down completely before God.

"It is your life, Lord," he said brokenly. "I give it back to You. Do whatever You want with me."

Since his parents had moved, he had rented a room in a private home and was doing his own cooking. The McLeroy and Fox families agreed to use part of their tithe to support him, giving the money through the church. In Japan nobody was familiar with that method of giving or of having to depend on others. Akitoshi was willing to try, but he was skeptical of the way it would work out.

Everything seemed to be all right until Roger and Margaret Fox went on a month's vacation in August. While they were around, Akitoshi had a measure of security. With them gone, even for a short time, he felt the future to be as uncertain as sand beneath his feet. He didn't realize it, but in his experience he was putting his trust in the missionaries when it should have been in God.

During this period he wrote to another American couple he learned to know during their stay in Japan with Youth For Christ.

"I am ashamed of it now," he told me only a few months ago, "but I wrote, complaining bitterly. If you must know the truth, I was worse than Jonah when God repented and spared Nineveh.

"As far as I was concerned, the missionaries had treated me shamefully. They had encouraged me to trust the Lord for my support. Then they had gone off and left me. I was out of money and was going to have to pawn my watch. When those few yen were gone, I didn't know what I would do. I didn't have enough to live on."

His American friends sent ten dollars to the Foxes by return mail and said they were going to send twenty-five dollars a month for his support. In those days before inflation, that was enough to take care of his needs.

About a year after he began to serve the Lord full time, he enrolled in the Japan Christian College. God was still dealing with him, and eventually he reached the place where he was able to surrender self completely and to trust God for every need. The first thing he did after making that decision was to write his friends in America, apologizing to them for his lack of faith and asking their forgiveness for writing as he had.

"So, please do not send any more money," he told them. "I will trust the Lord to take care of me."

Their answer came back quickly. "It wasn't you who told us to send money for your support. It was the Lord. Until He tells us to stop sending it, we will continue to do so."

God finally had Akitoshi Tahara at the place where He could use him.

NINE

When I was released from the hospital following the operation and my stumps had healed, I went to be fitted with artificial limbs. I can never express the joy and exhilaration that ran through me as I stood on my new legs for the first time. Once more I saw the world in its proper perspective.

I had been walking on my knees for so long I had forgotten what it was like to stand erect. Everything had been too big or too high for me. I couldn't help wash and dry the dishes. I had trouble turning on the lights, and whenever I wanted to go somewhere, I had to have help.

Now I was like a child who had miraculously grown to adulthood in an instant. I could see and reach things others could see and reach. I was able to hold my body straight and tall, and it would not be long until I would be taking care of myself. It was a marvelous feeling.

Akitoshi and I had been invited to the Foxes for dinner. When we finished eating, Margaret helped me to stand and was trying to help me learn to walk on my new legs. I teetered uncertainly across the floor to the kitchen sink. There were some unwashed dishes piled there and suddenly I realized I had to do something. Leaning against the counter for support, I began to wash the dishes. Excitedly, Akitoshi came over and began to dry them.

Roger got out his camera and photographed us. I still look on that moment as one of the happiest of my life.

It wasn't long, however, until my stumps ached, and sharp, incisive cramps tormented leg muscles that had grown flabby from lack of use. Still, I was reluctant to take off my legs. Hours passed before the pain subsided enough to allow me to sleep, but I was not disturbed by that.

"I can walk again!" I told myself, ignoring the throbbing agony that still wracked my stumps and thighs and back. "Praise God. I can walk! There are people who have their own legs but cannot get around on them. My legs are gone, yet I can walk! I can never complain again, no matter how painful it might be." I wanted to shout to the world, "God is so gracious and so good! I can walk!"

The science of making artificial limbs is not as advanced in Japan as it is in America and certain other parts of the world. My legs, though they were more costly than we had even imagined they could be, were so cumbersome and poorly made that I had difficulty adjusting to them. It seemed as though someone was always taking me to have them fitted or worked over.

"You have to remember these aren't your own legs," the limb-maker would explain, his exasperation escaping the thin curtain of his smile. "It takes time to learn to use them."

My family had even more difficulty in understanding that than I did. They were happy I had them but could not see the importance of helping me use them every day, exercising until the muscles were able to accept the harsh demands made by those clumsy artificial limbs. Margaret Fox realized what was happening and insisted that I move in with them for a time.

"You need help with your new legs every day," she said. "I'm afraid you'll get so discouraged that you'll give up before you've mastered them."

She was right about the discouragement. It was heavy upon me, a great, oppressive weight that seemed to quench my spirit. I am not sure what the Foxes honestly thought about having me live in their home, but it was a traumatic experience for me. I loved them. I still do. But I was raised in a culture as foreign to theirs as light is from darkness.

From my first recollection as a child, I had been taught that it was a virtue to suppress my emotions. I learned to mask my joy and pain, my love and displeasure, from others. I was trained not to cry in public or make any outward show of affection. I could never remember having my mother kiss me or tell me she loved me. I did not know what it was to feel my father's arm in love around me.

Suddenly I was thrust into a home with people who were warm and affectionate, people who had learned to demonstrate their love. Margaret treated me as she did her own daughter. She caressed me casually whenever she happened to be close to me, and I cringed inwardly. I had been around their home enough to know this was how she was—how they were. It used to bother me to see Roger put his arm around her or give her a quick kiss, as though I was glimpsing a scene that should take place in the bedroom. After a time I realized this was just the way they were with each other. I even came to accept that—for them. Having Margaret hug me was something else. I was never able to get used to it. I used to pray that God would help me to keep her from knowing how I actually felt about such demonstrations of love.

When I finally learned to walk on my new legs with some degree of stability, I moved back home. I missed the fellowship with the Foxes, but it was so comfortable being back with my family that I was even happier than before. I knew what they were thinking; I knew how they would react in almost every situation. Their ways were my ways. I found it much more to my liking than the strange openness of the Foxes.

For some reason discouragement was never far from me in those days. "I know we are not going to get married, Akitoshi," I would say, "so I don't want to go on seeing you. Please do not come to my home anymore."

Had he been as uncertain as I was, our marriage would never have become a reality. But it was as though he had special confidence from the Lord.

"God has led us together," he would tell me. "He has given us the same verse to show us He has placed His blessing on our plans. We are going to be married, Yoneko."

I found strength in his determination, but Mrs. McLeroy is the one who gave me the courage to continue seeing Akitoshi. She told both of us about a blind woman she knew in the States who fell in love and was married.

She went on to tell how concerned the couple was when they learned they were going to have a baby. They asked God to help her take care of the little one who would soon be with them. Her husband could not be home all the time; he had to go out to his job. And they did not have money enough to hire someone else to look after their child.

"When she tried to feed the baby," Mrs. McLeroy said, "she found that she didn't have to search for the baby's mouth. She would hold out a spoonful of food, and the baby would come to the spoon. She had no problem changing diapers or doing any of the other jobs that have to be done when you have a tiny baby to care for. Oh, she had difficulty at first. She had to learn to do things differently than most women because of her blindness, but even in those things God guided her. Soon she was as competent as any young mother and had complete confidence in her ability to care for her little one as well as any mother with two good eyes.

"After a year or so, she and her husband learned of a doctor who had developed an operation to correct her type of blindness. She had it done and regained her sight. When they had another child, he was ordinary in every way. He lacked the ability to help his mother. She did not need the special assistance she did when she was blind, so God did not provide it.

"This didn't happen because God loved my blind friend better than anyone else. It is only an example of how He supplies special grace wherever it is needed in our lives. He will do the same for you and Andy. Keep on trusting the Lord for the wisdom and strength you need. You're making it all right. And if you feel God is leading you to marry Andy, don't hesitate because of your legs. God will help you to overcome that handicap, too."

I was strangely touched by that story. It quieted the fears of my heart. I had been concerned about having babies and caring for them. That was one of the reasons I was determined not to marry. I knew Akitoshi loved children. And if we were to be married I wanted a family. Hearing about Mrs. McLeroy's blind friend gave me courage.

And why shouldn't I believe God would work for me the same as He had for the woman who could not see? Hadn't He kept me alive when I longed for death? Hadn't He brought Akitoshi and the missionaries to the hospital to tell me about Himself when I hated Him? Hadn't He given us the same verse as a seal of His approval of our marriage?

I began to plan for marriage hopefully, resting in God's promise to meet my needs.

I can't say my doubts disappeared or that I no longer feared the responsibilities of marrying. There were still times when I was sure I could never go through with it, when I longed to have Akitoshi go away and not come back. It was not that I doubted my love for him. I could not bear to think of life without him. Yet, he was the source of the turmoil and anguish that plagued me. With him gone, I would be spared the agony of such a decision as I now faced.

But he was not gone. He was always there, a step or two away it seemed, trying to anticipate any need of mine, any desire he could help provide. I could not help myself. We were married and moved into a little garage-type building that was at one time used for keeping cattle and horses.

Akitoshi was reluctant to take me there.

"It is not very large," he said.

"But it is a house of our own."

"Hai," he acknowledged. "It is a place of our own." Then, fearing he was giving me the wrong impression and I would be disappointed when I saw it, he added quickly, "Perhaps I had better say it is a building where we will be living. You could hardly call it a house."

My gaze narrowed. "A store building?" I asked.

"Not exactly," he stammered. "It's sort of like a small barn."

"A barn?" I echoed. "You can't be serious."

"It's really too small for a barn. I guess you would have to say it's a shed."

There! It was out! Fearfully his gaze met mine. He was wondering what I was thinking, what I would say.

"But it hasn't been used for animals for a long time," he blurted. "It's been cleaned out, and it's painted quite nicely. We can paint it again if you wish."

I was too happy to protest, too excited to find anything wrong. Akitoshi and I were married and would be spending the rest of our lives together. That was all that mattered.

He had always been able to do everything, in my eyes. He could answer practically any question about the Bible. He could talk with the missionaries about any subject they cared to discuss, and if they needed anything fixed they always called on him. If he had chosen the home or barn or shed or whatever we were renting, it was nice enough for us. If it wasn't, he would make it livable. I had complete confidence in his ability.

The place we moved into was smaller than I had anticipated. There was one room on the main floor about the size of a garage for a Datsun or a Honda or a Toyota. There was a tiny kitchen in one corner and an attic half the size of the room below. We could only stand up in the center, under the peak.

I looked the house over and giggled. "It looks like a doll-house, *Anata,*" I told him, using the term many wives used in addressing their husbands.

He looked at me and laughed. The tension was broken. He knew the little house would be our home without complaint. It is true my training as a child was such that I would never have raised my voice against it. Yet Akitoshi was so sensitive to my moods that he would have known my dislike immediately.

I can honestly say the size of the house did not matter to me. A mansion near the palace in Tokyo, a lavish apartment in one of the new high-rises, or a shed first built for cows or parking cars in a village five miles from Hachioji City were all the same to me.

I had my Lord Jesus Christ who saved me, Akitoshi who loved me, and I could walk. My heart echoed and reechoed the Hallelujah Chorus. I could walk! Can you wonder why I praise Him? Can you see why I considered myself the wealthiest of women?

It was necessary for us to live as inexpensively as possible. Akitoshi was still going to school, and we were living on the gifts from concerned believers. There was seldom more than enough money to meet our most pressing needs.

I was caught up in my effort to learn how to cook and to clean our little home without calling on Akitoshi or one of the missionaries. Once we were living together, I soon realized that he was not as perfect as I had imagined when I first met him. He left his clothes where he got out of them. When I mentioned it to him, he was contrite and promised to do better. Strangely, he was never able to remember in the morning what he had promised so earnestly the night before. I learned it was easier to devise ways of picking up after him than to get him to do it himself.

While Akitoshi was away at school or working in the mission-operated bookstore in Yokohama, I began to discover how I could perform the menial little household tasks that the average woman does without ever thinking about them.

Peeling a potato was particularly difficult until I discovered how to do it. I could have asked Akitoshi to do it for me. He was always quick to help, but I didn't like to bother him. My father always said I was the daughter of my mother. I had always been determined to take care of myself. Even as a child it galled me to have to seek help and I would fumble endlessly with a button when a word to one of the family would have solved the problem in a hurry.

I have always wanted to look nice and used to put my hair up regularly before my accident. Afterward Yuriko took care of it for me. Now, however, I was living in my own home and she was several miles away. After working endlessly at it, I learned I could roll up my hair as other women did and bend over to hold a curl in place while I inserted a bobby pin. It took me a little longer that way, but I could do it.

Each new skill—each new way of taking care of myself or our home—was a major achievement. For those who build planes or ships or control vast financial empires, my little accomplishments would seem ridiculous. To me, they were the milestones on the road to independence.

I earnestly sought God's guidance whenever some new situation troubled me. I thanked and praised Him when it was solved.

TEN

I was frightened when I first learned I was pregnant, and filled with dread in spite of our happiness at the prospect of having a family. I suppose most girls receive the news with torn emotions. There were the long, uncomfortable months of waiting and the ordeal of childbirth, mingled with the excitement of being God's instrument to bring a new life into the world.

With me it was more than that. I longed to bear Akitoshi's child and see a tiny replica of his gentle smile and shy, expressive eyes fixed lovingly on me. I ached for the warmth of a small body against my heart and soft little lips on my breast. But I also dreaded the responsibility, the endless demands a baby would make on me.

I had struggled for several days to master peeling a potato with two fingers and a thumb. How could I possibly do all the things I would have to do to take care of a little one? The wives of the American missionaries tried hard to make me believe I had nothing to worry about. It seemed to me they tried too hard, as though they were trying to convince themselves as well.

Even Akitoshi shrugged away the possibility of problems. "God will provide," he said casually, the way he always did when we lacked the funds to pay an approaching bill.

Actually, he was as disturbed as I was about the bewildering situation I had to face, and he prayed much for me. But I didn't know that. I read his careless remark as a lack of concern. And I was furious at him for one of the few times since

I had known him. I wanted to shout at him, to fling his easy assurance of my ability into his teeth.

It was simple enough for him to talk, I raged inwardly. I was the one who would have to cope with taking care of a baby with only one arm and two legs that were not my own. I was the one who would have to struggle with each new situation, not only learning what had to be done but figuring some way to do it. For a time I was again overwhelmed with self-pity. I was sure I was the only young woman in all of Japan who faced such problems.

But I did not voice my anger. I buried it deep inside and hid it behind a waxen smile. As always, however, Akitoshi read my confusion and hurt and bewilderment. When he came home the next afternoon, he had a copy of Dr. Spock's book on baby care. I don't know where he was able to get it.

"It's in English," I protested when he gave it to me.

"I know, but I'll translate for you."

Love for him filled my eyes and for an instant, before I fought it down, I wanted to lay my head against his chest and sob out my frustration and fear. But that was not proper, so I sat down obediently and listened while he read from the book in English and gave me a rough Japanese translation. My own problems I would have to face in my own way, learning to diaper a baby with two fingers and a thumb, giving a helpless little one a bath, and carrying her without dropping her. I would have to figure out how to hold my baby and give her medicine and how to wash for her and do all the other demanding tasks of being a mother. But from the baby book and Akitoshi I learned all the things I did not know.

During those long weeks I think I loved my husband more than ever before. I was confident God had provided exactly the right man for me. He knew everything and had the love and tenderness to quiet any ache in my heart.

I have realized, before and since, that he was not quite perfect. Discouragement came easily to him, and there were times when he lacked the understanding I seemed to need so desperately. At that moment, however, the eyes of love dimmed any faults I had seen in him. He was a man of infinite patience, and flawless in his kindness and compassion.

The last weeks of pregnancy are always a nightmare for an expectant mother. For me they were particularly difficult. I had the same ugly, ponderous stomach I thought would never become normal again, the same constant heaviness, the same aching back. I didn't feel sick, only constantly uncomfortable. I also had the added difficulty of maneuvering my swollen, unbalanced body on artificial legs. I dreaded getting up in the morning to fix breakfast for Akitoshi. I dreaded cleaning our little home. Even a delightful event like going to church was an agony to be endured. I thought my confinement would never end.

However, Akitoshi was looking toward the day I would have to get to the hospital. He said nothing because he didn't want to frighten me, but I could tell he was disturbed. He was away most of every day. If the pains started when he was at work or at school, he had to be sure I could get help.

He knew the fire department furnished ambulance service, so he went to see about it. Yes, they had an ambulance we could call. Yes, they would be glad to get me to the hospital, even as far away as the Adventist hospital where I had reservations. Akitoshi was relieved and arranged for a neighbor to notify the fire station if that was necessary.

Although the plans were made, God apparently didn't want me to go to the hospital alone. In His kindness and mercy He saw to it that Akitoshi was with me. He knew, even better than I, that I needed my husband.

I had an appointment with the doctor on Sunday afternoon, the day before our baby was due. It was an unusual day for a doctor's appointment but the obstetrician practiced at the Adventist hospital where Sunday was a working day. In one way it was good for us. Akitoshi was busy during the week with school and his job at the mission bookstore. It was difficult for him to get away, even for an afternoon.

As we got ready to leave the house, I didn't feel much different than I had the past two weeks. I had slept poorly the night before and experienced a few deep, driving pains in my lower abdomen, but they had stopped shortly after we got up. I was really no more uncomfortable than I had been for some time.

Akitoshi took me to the railway station on his bicycle. He sat on the seat and pedaled while I rode on the padded carrier behind, balancing my ungainly figure and hanging on as best I could. Although I don't remember it, people must have turned around and looked at us as we rode those two miles on Akitoshi's bicycle and parked it in the racks at the station.

The doctor examined me and suggested that we walk around the block. When we got back, she said the baby was due the next day and it would be wise for me to check in right away. Akitoshi watched me closely to see if I was afraid, but God had given me complete victory and peace. I didn't know how I would be able to take care of a baby, but I had the assurance God would provide the help and wisdom I needed. Like Akitoshi said, I was expecting a miracle. I saw not one miracle but many the next few months as I struggled to learn to care for our little one.

Marie was born without difficulty, and I recovered rapidly. In ten days we were home, the same as other mothers and their babies. Akitoshi went over the baby book with me once more, and I made a few notes.

Since he was going to school and working with the missionaries, we never had more than just enough money to get those things we absolutely had to have. Our only furniture was a small used portable-type closet which Akitoshi had bought for our clothes, a little table, and a small cupboard in the kitchen. We didn't even have enough money to buy a chest of drawers for Marie's things. He brought home a number of apple boxes and made shelves of them. He painted them nicely, and I made curtains for them of some material one of the missionaries gave me.

The only new clothes we had for her were a couple of dozen American-type diapers sent by our friends in the States. The rest were things the missionaries gave us that their own children had outgrown.

The wife of one of the teachers at the Christian Academy loaned us a bathinette. It was a little plastic tub on a stand with a top that came down or went up when I stepped on the peddle. I could lay Marie on it to undress her, lift her up, and raise the top out of the way with my foot so I could put her in the tub. When I had finished, I could take her out of the water, lower the top, and have a convenient place to lay her where I could dry her and dress her. It was an ideal device for me.

By this time both the Foxes and the McLeroys had left Japan, and there was no car available to take Marie and me home. However, our friends from the school came with their little car and got us.

The young nurse who came to get Marie ready to leave the hospital had never seen American baby clothes before. She got her out of the outfit the hospital supplied, but that was as far as she could go. She held up the strange gown in complete bewilderment.

"Here," Akitoshi said, "I know how to do it."

That surprised her. I suppose she had never seen a man dress a baby before. Even I was surprised at his skill.

"I used to baby-sit for some American friends," he explained.

When we were alone, he told me this was one more way God had worked to help us. There were times when he had felt the Foxes were imposing upon him by asking him to take care of their children. Actually, however, it had been a period of training. He learned to change diapers, give their baby a bath, and feed her. Now he was able to teach me.

When we got back to the house, the missionary teacher's wife showed us how to use the bathinette. That was actually all the help we ever had.

The next day, as soon as Akitoshi went to work, I determined to give Marie a bath by myself. I had the heater going until the house was unusually warm, then moved the bathinette into our tiny kitchen beside the sink. I was a little uneasy as I got her undressed. I needn't have been. It took me longer than it would have taken a mother with two hands, but I managed very well.

When Akitoshi came home that night, I was ecstatic.

"I bathed her all by myself. It was so easy. And she enjoyed it just like a grown-up person!"

I don't believe either of us had ever experienced such happiness, except for the day we became believers in Jesus Christ and the day we were married. For a long while we lay in each others' arms praising God for the way He was taking care of us.

"It's just like the missionaries said," I murmured. "God is helping me just as He helped the blind woman."

Our landlord was as amazed as I was. "I seldom hear your baby cry," he would tell us. "And she seems so happy. How is that?"

It was always that way with Marie. When I went to diaper her, she would lie very still and hold her little legs up until I finished. When I dressed her, she was patient, even though I had trouble with the buttons and fasteners. And when I held her in my arm, it wasn't long until she would put her little arms around my neck and cling to me.

There were times when Akitoshi was very discouraged. There were so many things we needed and so little money for them that he felt as though he wasn't fulfilling his obligation as a husband and father. For several months the only income we had was $50.00 a month that came from the States. It was difficult to pay all of our bills, especially during those weeks when our funds were slow in coming. Still, we took our tithe out of every check before we bought anything for ourselves.

"We must give that which belongs to God to Him first," Akitoshi said.

After that we took out the money it would cost for powdered milk for Marie. We lived on what was left. Never once did we go hungry, but there were times when we thought we would. We didn't always have money enough to ride the train to church and still have anything left for the offering. When that happened, Akitoshi would take Marie and me on the bicycle, peddling four or five miles, half of which was over gravel roads. Marie was seven months old when we first made the trip by bicycle, but she clung so tightly to me I never once was afraid I would drop her.

When she was two years old, she was at the stage where she liked to watch water, especially when I was washing dishes. She was constantly at my side, standing on a little stool and peeking under my arm. It didn't matter that she was splashed in the face now and then. She loved it.

One evening I had finished the dishes and was washing the pans. A large aluminum kettle gave me trouble. I couldn't hold it and scrub it at the same time. As soon as Marie saw what was happening, she grasped it with her chubby fingers and held it so I could wash it. I was amazed and felt the very presence of the Lord beside me.

Akitoshi was away at a meeting, as he often was at night, and I waited up for him. I usually had tea ready and we would have something to eat while we shared what had happened since we had been apart. That evening I could scarcely wait until he got home to tell him what had happened.

"When Marie reached out her hand to help me," I told him breathlessly, "I felt as though Jesus was standing here beside me, telling me He was showing me how carefully He was going to look after me. I could almost hear Him say, 'See, your little one is not a burden to you. She is a help.' It was so precious!"

For a long while after I finished, Akitoshi was silent. And when he spoke he quoted a Bible verse: *"My grace is sufficient for thee."**

We made several moves as Akitoshi's work took him to different places. When Marie was five, we were living in a small house up five or six concrete steps from the graveled road. The road was rough and hilly, which made it difficult for me to walk. I didn't like that. I enjoyed meeting people and visiting with them, and I didn't want to spend all of my time inside.

So Marie would go with me. The first time we went to the store fifty yards away, she walked down the steps at my side. On the rough road she turned to me, seeming to sense that I was afraid of falling.

"I will walk in front, Mama," she said. "I will be strong. Hold onto my neck, and I will be your cane."

No matter how often she went with me, I was never afraid of falling. She did become my good, strong cane.

The house we were living in had a small wooden balcony around a front window. It was too small for an adult, but

*2 Corinthians 12:9.

Marie made it a favorite perch. She would sit with her feet stuck between the posts on the railing and watch people go by.

"Hello," she would call out in her thin baby voice. "How are you?"

They soon learned her name and would look for her as they went by. "Hello, Marie-san," they would say. "How are you?"

It amused me to go shopping with her. I might be a stranger, but everybody seemed to know Marie. They would come up and talk with her. It made it easy for me to talk with them, too.

One of the town leaders told Akitoshi he had seen me almost every day for a year before he realized I was handicapped. He didn't even notice I only had one arm.

About the same time an elderly woman who lived next door questioned Marie about me. She was deaf, and their loud voices penetrated the thin walls of our house.

"Doesn't your mother have her arm?"

"No," Marie said as naturally as though she was asking if we had tea in the afternoon. "She doesn't have her arm. She doesn't even have any legs."

I don't know what the old lady said in return, but Marie continued proudly. "But you know, Grandma, she made this dress for me with her one arm. She does everything so well."

After Ruth was born, Marie was there to help me, although a little jealousy showed through at times. When the baby had a bottle, she wanted one. I solved the problem by giving her a glass with a little milk in it whenever Ruth was fed.

More significant was the difference in the temperaments of the two girls. Marie was a model baby who seemed to sense what to do to help me take care of her. Ruth was never difficult to manage, but she was more like other babies. She kicked and twisted during diapering and squirmed when I tried to fasten or free the buttons on her clothes. God knew I needed special help with Marie. By the time Ruth came along, I was experienced and self-assured. And I had Marie to help me in so many ways.

When I read again the story of God giving the manna to the children of Israel, I could not help thinking how similar it was to my experience. God gave them only the manna they would need for each day. If they tried to gather more, it was wormy and unfit to eat the next morning. He gave me the help I needed in caring for Marie. Now that the need for special assistance was gone, our next baby was like any other.

ELEVEN

Although the birth of our daughters had brought new problems for me, I had many earlier difficulties to face and solve in keeping a home before the girls came along.

Both Akitoshi and I had been raised in homes that were much nicer than the one we were able to afford when we were first married. The furnishings had been much more convenient and comfortable, and our parents had been able to afford whatever they wanted to eat. We were young, however, and serving the Lord. Even before we were married, we realized we would not have as much as other young couples. The area we lived in was respectable, and our farmer neighbors were friendly people. We were happy in spite of our lack of nice things. Or, as Akitoshi often said, perhaps material things contribute little to happiness. We had nothing, but we were happy.

I can't say I was completely satisfied with our little home. It never stopped looking like a stable to me, and with good reason. It had been a stable.

It wasn't painted on the inside. As I recall, it was paneled with veneered plywood. Half the kitchen floor was covered with wood, the other half was dirt. And we had to carry the water we used.

Akitoshi could not stand having me live like that. From our meager income he bought boards to cover the dirt portion of the floor and painted them. He also got permission to run a hose from the spring behind our place into the house and to the kitchen sink. The water ran constantly, but that was better than having to bucket it in. We heated with a little cast-iron coal stove of uncertain vintage or origin. We would light a fire every morning for an hour or two in the winter when it was cold, but we were not able to keep it burning all the time. The cost of coal was too great for our straining budget.

Long before we moved there, a Japanese toilet had been installed in the northwest corner of the converted stable where it would be fairly cool. It was a traditional Japanese toilet, an oval piece of white china with a hole in it, put in at ground level. I couldn't use such a toilet so Akitoshi remodeled it, setting it on a platform about the height of a Western toilet. I have often wondered what the next tenants thought when they saw it.

Those first months of marriage were difficult for both Akitoshi and me. After those first glorious days when nothing could go wrong, we settled into the routine of regular living. I can see now that a major source of frustration came from my childish fantasy that Akitoshi was perfect. I expected far too much from him. In my eyes he was on a towering pinnacle far above anyone else I knew. He could not possibly have stayed on it. As I got to know him more intimately and saw that his halo was beginning to slip, I was shattered. He was actually human with human faults.

The man who never hung up anything in our little house, whose socks were always wrong side out in the middle of the floor, whose shirts could be found in any corner, this man couldn't be the man I married.

There was another side to his quiet, thoughtful nature that my father admired very much. He was shy and introverted. Meeting new people was difficult for him, and he was content to stay at home whenever he could. I wanted to be with people. Frequently he was discouraged and unhappy. If a pet project was delayed or he encountered unexpected difficulties, he was sure success would never come. The problems he faced were always blacker than those of anyone else.

As for me, I had been spoiled outrageously by an indulgent mother. My older sister, Yuriko, learned to cook and clean and sew and was expected to assume certain duties around the house. As the youngest, as well as the most favored daughter, little was expected of me. I hadn't even been aware of the harm that sort of treatment did to me until we were married. When I tried to take over in the kitchen, I soon discovered there was very little I could do except to wash dishes and make tea. But I was fiercely determined to learn.

The first argument we had was over Akitoshi's insistence that he help me in the kitchen. He smothered me with attention and attempted to do everything for me. I thought at the time that he did it because he pitied me. Now I wonder if he didn't pity himself because of the poor food I was putting in his stomach.

Few men are as well equipped to cook as he was. He had helped in a restaurant for a time and cooked for himself for a couple of years. He even knew how to make pickles, something many women can't do. So he puttered around in the kitchen, doing things that I should have been doing for myself. Finally I lost my temper.

"Please, Akitoshi!" I snapped bitterly. "If I want your help, I'll ask for it. Just leave me alone!"

It was three years before he wiped a dish or cleaned or cooked.

I may have been jealous of his skill in the kitchen, and I was frustrated for knowing so little, but those were not my only reasons for insisting on doing the work myself. Shortly after my release from the hospital, I had discovered that I was developing a tendency to sit back and let others do things for me. If I hesitated as I was about to get up on my knees and go to the kitchen for something, Yuriko would jump up and get it for me. If I was going to change my clothes, she was there to help me. If I grew weary doing the few little tasks assigned to me, she would whip through them in a fraction of the time they would take me. I was feeling increasingly helpless and very sorry for myself.

After a time I saw that I was going to spend the rest of my life as a burden to those I loved the most unless I learned to take care of myself. Something deep within me rebelled at that. And with it a fierce determination to do all that others did took hold of me. Like my mother after her first stroke, I decided I wasn't going to be waited on like a child. When Akitoshi and I first began to talk of marriage, I was even more firm in my resolve to learn how to keep my home the way any other wife would expect to.

At first I was not aware that God was in my new independence. As I began to keep house, however, I saw His hand in my own desires. I longed to do everything other wives did, but I could not without the help of God. He wanted to show me how to accomplish each simple little job so I could see how much He loved me. I didn't want to miss those special blessings.

Even a little matter like peeling potatoes was too difficult for me without His help. I tried to hold the potato in place with my thumb and hold the knife with my fingers but it wouldn't work. The potato went around and around as I struggled with the peeling. I took another and began again, but the contrary vegetable popped from under my thumb and fell to the floor. I was close to tears as I looked down at it.

"There's no use trying," I reasoned. "I'll never be able to do it." Then I remembered the many ways in which God had guided me, supplying my need when I could not take care of myself.

"I can't do it!" I cried out to Him. "You've got to help me!"

I hadn't finished praying when God gave me a wonderful idea. I knew it would work even before I tried it. I cut another potato in half and put the flat side on the cutting board. It was simple, then, to hold it in place while I peeled it.

I learned to hold bottles between my knees or under my chin to open them. And later, when Marie came along, I used my mouth or my stump to tie ribbons in her hair.

I could never remember how many times God has answered my quick, fervent prayers for help as I faced a situation I didn't know how to cope with. My greatest handicaps have also been my greatest source of blessing. I have had the opportunity to develop a complete dependence upon God that comes to few individuals.

Yet, there were times when I did some very foolish things. As a boy growing up in downtown Tokyo, Akitoshi had fish often and grew up liking all sorts of seafood. Our family seldom had fish, and when we did my father removed the bones and cut up my serving. I didn't even know how to eat fish without help, let alone prepare them.

Then Akitoshi came home with some seafood.

"We're going to have fried oysters tonight," he said, studying me carefully. "I hope you'll be able to cook them."

I think he wanted to help, or at least to tell me how, but I was too proud and independent for that. I was his wife. It was my responsibility to cook for him, even slimy, unappetizing food like oysters.

When he came home that night, dinner was ready and I was quite proud of myself. I had managed to fry the oysters without his help. He asked the blessing and then he raised his head and studied the little fried morsels on his plate. I could see the question in his eyes, but I thought he was marveling at my accomplishment. He took a bite, chewed it slowly, and swallowed. With his chopsticks poised above his plate, he finally voiced his puzzlement.

"What is this you've served tonight, Yoneko? I thought we were going to have the oysters."

"It is oysters." By this time I was defensive.

"What in the world did you do to them?"

"I washed them first," I told him. I was surprised he didn't know that would have to be done. "Then I noticed they still didn't look so good, so I took away all the insides and saved the good parts!"

For a long while he looked at me, the strangest expression on his face.

"Yoneko," he said quietly, "if we *ever* have fried oysters again, I am going to prepare them."

I did learn to cook eventually, although I am sure there were some meals when we were first married that were quite difficult for Akitoshi to swallow. Graciously, however, he refrained from calling my attention to them.

I liked to bake cookies and often fixed some to take to our landlord's family. They had many sons and daughters, but they allowed us to use their bath, and I appreciated it. We had no bath in our tiny house. The farmer's bath was half outside, and in the winter it was breezy and cold, but we enjoyed it.

During the year or more we lived there, we got well acquainted with the young farm couple who lived across the street. We started a Bible study in our home and invited them to come. The husband either did not grasp the message of Jesus Christ or was determined not to yield to it. His wife, however, became very interested. Before we moved I had the privilege of praying with her to receive Christ. I have kept in touch with her since and her faith has been growing steadily.

Such a victory should have been encouraging to me. In a way it was, but I had times of emptiness and despondency. Money was a continual problem, and I was more disturbed by Akitoshi's frequent periods of discouragement than I let him know. He felt the long train ride to and from work in the Yokohama bookstore was a waste of valuable time. Actually, he thought the entire assignment was wasting his education and training.

"I shouldn't have to stay there and do such work," he complained to me. "I am trained to preach. I'd like to have a church."

Eventually he was given a small church to pastor, and we moved so we could be closer to it. But before that happened, I came face to face with the reality of living the Christian life. I longed to serve God in a more important way. I had taught a Sunday school class previously, and I wanted to teach again and to be active in serving God in other ways where exciting things were happening. I used to pray a lot that God would use me in ways that would permit me to do more for Him.

That was the situation when a close friend from Australia came to hold a Bible conference for the missionaries. He was not actually a member of the Far Eastern Gospel Crusade, with which we had aligned ourselves, but he spoke often to our group and had many friends among our people.

I was as depressed as ever, but as the conference approached, a significant change crept into my thinking. God was once more speaking to my heart, telling me I was blaming others for my unhappiness when I should have looked within. It was my fault I was depressed. I needed to give the Holy Spirit complete control of my life.

It was not easy for one like myself to accept such a revelation without fighting against it, and fight I did. But the gnawing emptiness persisted and I began to look forward eagerly to the meetings.

I had missed quite a few services the past couple of months and used our daughter as my excuse. But now I wanted to go to the meetings. There was never anyone to leave Marie with, so we took her along. That night the speaker was talking to all of the missionary wives, but I thought he was only talking to me.

When the service was over, I told Akitoshi I had to talk to the speaker. We stayed behind, and he patiently showed me what God wanted me to know. But first he got me to talk, to open my heart and share what had been churning there, unspoken.

It all came out—my despondency at being unable to serve the Lord as I wanted to; my disillusionment with Akitoshi at seeing how far from ideal he really was. It hurt him to have me give voice to my frustration before our friend. I could read it in his solemn, kind eyes. It hurt me to have to say such things about one whom I loved so deeply. But it had to be spoken. No longer could I keep my feelings hidden in the dark, cold recesses of my heart where they could fester and rankle in silent resentment. I had to get them out where they could be seen and, in some way, resolved.

When I finished, our friend began to share God's Word with me as carefully as though I were an audience of a thousand or ten thousand. He spoke slowly, giving me time to savor each sentence, each phrase, each word.

"God doesn't hold you responsible for what you do as a wife, Yoneko," he told me, "as long as you are obedient to your husband. God's will for you as a housewife is not primarily to win souls. He hasn't called you to teach Sunday school at the expense of your duties as a wife and mother. Now, God may want you to teach Sunday school, but your primary responsibility is to be obedient to your husband."

Even though I had been raised in the traditional Japanese way and had been taught as a child that my husband would one day be my master, even as my father was my mother's master while she lived, it was not easy for me to accept those words. Becoming a believer had not removed my desire for independence.

"Your husband may be discouraging to you because he does not live up to all the things you thought he was before the two of you were married, but that should not make any difference in your relationship to him. God wants you to be obedient and to be a good mother to your baby. You can be completely confident you are in the will of the Lord if you do these things. If you can't go out as often as you like to witness, or stay as long as you think you should when you are able to go, don't fret about it. If you are really concerned about souls, God will bring needy people to your house door, to your room. Don't worry, Yoneko. He will give you many, many opportunities to witness for Him."

I was not alone in being close to tears. I looked up at Akitoshi with swimming eyes and saw that he, too, was about to cry silently. There were also tears in the eyes of Joseph Caroll, our tender, understanding friend. I knew God was meeting with us, and the others felt the same.

"There are some portions of Scripture I would like to have you read," he said, opening my Bible to the third chapter of 1 Peter. "Likewise, ye wives, be in subjection to your own husbands."*

When I finished there, he had me turn to Ephesians 5:22-33, where I read what a wife is expected to be.

"I—I never realized before what God wants me to do," I I stammered.

Bowing my head, I confessed my wrong attitude before the Lord. I told Him how sorry I was that I had allowed myself to be frustrated, that I complained about my husband and wanted him to do things my way.

*1 Peter 3:1.

As I prayed, God removed all the cancerous ugliness I had been clutching to my heart, and a wonderful peace came over me. My very being overflowed with joy. From that time on I had a new attitude toward being a wife and mother. I found joy in cooking and sewing and cleaning house.

Years later, both of our daughters were to say they had never seen me cry because of unhappiness, nor had they ever heard me complain. I can take no credit for that. It stems from the change God brought into my life that night when I yielded completely to Him.

Pastor Caroll had told me God would send people to me so I would be able to speak to them of Him. I prayed that He might, but I was prepared to spend my life in the background, taking care of our home and baby if that was what He wanted me to do. It was exactly as our friend said it would be. God gave me more chances to witness than I had ever had before.

We had a Bible study in our home with good results; and wherever I went about the neighborhood, I had opportunities to share my faith. When I went to the grocery store, which was almost daily, I handed tracts to those people I met: to newsboys, wives, and an occasional farmer. The people began to ask questions, and I was able to tell them about our marvelous Lord.

There were to be other situations that allowed me to witness for my Lord and Saviour far beyond our home and our little Japanese village, but it seems as though God did not want me to know of that yet. He wanted to work in my heart until I was willing to place myself completely in His hands.

TWELVE

*We were finally given a small church which Akitoshi pas*tored for a time before God called us to Minobu at the foot of Mount Fuji's western slope. The city of 10,000 is holy ground for devout Buddhists, with the roots of the entire community plunged deeply into that ancient religion. It reaches back to a radical saffron-robed priest who roamed the mountain villages and towns and cities several hundred years ago, preaching boldly against the corrupt government of the day. Countless numbers were attracted by his fierce courage and honesty, and they flocked to join the Buddhist sect he founded. Many donated vast lands and money to build the magnificent temple at Minobu as the center of their faith. Today the entire town, built on what was once temple land, encircles the temple like a wheel circles its hub, and temples have sprouted everywhere. It is a city of temples that continues to beckon to Buddhist pilgrims.

Entire planeloads of faithful worshipers descend on Minobu from all over the country. Even larger crowds come by bus or train. The area has become one of the most popular meccas for devout Buddhists to be found anywhere in Japan.

Unnoticed by the hordes of the faithful who are regularly disgorged on the community from high-speed trains is the building that housed the only Christian church. It is nestled behind the railway station in an inconspicuous spot as though it has some reason to hide.

Few would have thought about it had they caught a glimpse of it and recognized it for what it was. Few of the local residents knew it was there, nor would they have been impressed had they been informed of its existence. They were completely disillusioned with all forms of religion.

The Buddhist tourist from outside the little mountain valley finds Minobu serene and beautiful, a place he will remember all his life. Even the casual nonreligious visitor is sure to be impressed by what he sees. The town, which devotes most of its energy to taking care of the pilgrim, presents a pretty picture of tranquility.

To the people who live there, it has an ugliness all its own. They do not see the ornate splendor of the temples or the charm of smiling, shaven-headed priests. They know those are but the trappings of piety that have been carefully constructed to hide the truth. They know the temples own the hotels and eating places and souvenir shops, and that the priests and their concubines, who can control those businesses, soon become wealthy. And they know about the deadly infighting that constantly goes on for control of the more profitable enterprises, and the evil tactics which supposedly holy men will employ.

Most of the residents of Minobu regarded Christianity with the same contempt, so the struggling little church was ignored by most of those who were aware that it existed. A few old people and the missionaries came to the ordinary family-type dwelling that had been rented to serve as a place for the little group to meet. That was all.

Akitoshi was invited to speak there on a Sunday shortly after Willard Reimer and his wife came to fill in for the former missionaries who had gone back to the States on furlough.

"Wouldn't it be nice if you folks could come here and help us?" Reimer joked. "The people have been praying for a pastor and we have been praying for someone to help us. Our church building is really a house, so we've even got a place for you to live."

He wasn't serious and neither were we. We all laughed about it. But God was speaking. It wasn't long until we were back at Minobu, remodeling the house to make it more comfortable for our little family.

I learned much while we were there. Few came to the services, but they were wonderful Christians. One evening as I started to prepare the evening meal, I realized that we only had potatoes and there was no money to buy anything else. I was praying as I worked. It isn't pleasant to have to prepare such a skimpy meal for a husband and two hungry children.

I hadn't finished peeling the potatoes when there was a Christian woman at the door with some food. "This afternoon God spoke to me about sharing what we have with you," she said. "We just had a fresh crop of rice, and when we finished harvesting, you were the first ones I thought of."

She and her husband were comparatively poor, but she brought us enough food to keep us going until our check arrived.

We also served another church in the same general area, and then after several years the Lord led us back to greater Tokyo where Akitoshi had been able to build a house for us.

I don't want to minimize my husband's work in this new location. God has always used him in ways that have thrilled us both, and this assignment was as fruitful as the others. But I have always felt that God moved us to that particular place at that particular time to keep a divine appointment, the way He moved Philip to go down to the Gaza Desert to talk with the eunuch.*

By that time Marie and Ruth were old enough to go to kindergarten and nursery school. Whenever there was a gathering of parents, Akitoshi would take me on the back of his motorcycle. God used those meetings to send a girl in her

*Acts 8:26-39.

late teens to me for help. She also had become so discouraged with life that she had jumped in front of a train.

For some reason Akitoshi was home the afternoon a car stopped in front of our house and an older woman and two girls came to the door. He invited the visitors in and I got cushions for them, wondering why such well-dressed women would come to our modest home. It was obvious they were nervous and ill at ease. The older woman fussed over one of the girls, the one with the sorrowing eyes who looked so much like her. After they left, Akitoshi said he had not seen anyone so sad since the first day he went to the hospital to visit my room.

Although the unhappy girl tried to hide it under the long sleeves of her kimono, I saw that her left arm had been amputated at the shoulder and her right hand was gone. My heart went out to her. I could still remember those difficult days when I was so ashamed I tried to hide the fact that I was handicapped.

The mother did the talking. It was unforgivable of them to come barging in on us the way they had, she began in the accepted manner of Japanese etiquette, but several of their friends had told them about me. Even though they couldn't learn my name and had a difficult time locating my address, they felt they had to come and see me.

"There is this young woman who comes to the meetings of the parents at school," their friends had related. "She is an amputee, yet she seems so happy and self-confident, we wonder if she might be able to help Tomiko-san."

"Life has been so miserable for poor Tomiko since—since her accident," the woman concluded. "We thought perhaps you might be able to help her."

My heart was praising God for this opportunity to share His love and strength and guidance with someone who faced the same difficulties I had. I knew the turmoil Tomiko-san was experiencing. I had gone through the same black, tortuous despair.

"I will be grateful for the chance to try." Turning to our handicapped guest, I began to question her about the things she had learned to do to take care of herself.

Self-pity trembled on her lips, and I soon learned her mother had an entirely different sort of help in mind. "She is able to do nothing for herself," she broke in almost accusingly, as though I was wrong in even suggesting such things. "I even have to feed her."

"You can learn to do that, Tomiko-san," I said.

"How can she?" her mother demanded belligerently. "She has no hands. I have to dress and undress her and help her use the toilet. She can't open or close a door or write a letter." She gestured helplessly. "She can't do anything for herself, and I have been with her every day since she was released from the hospital."

"I know it is difficult," I acknowledged, "but—"

"She is so unhappy," her mother informed us, cutting in before I was able to finish what I was saying. "We thought maybe you could help her to accept the terrible thing that has happened to her and help her to be happy and contented again."

I thought of talking with them about Jesus Christ and what He could do for all three of them, but the Holy Spirit wouldn't give me peace to do so, except in a general way. I showed them my stumps and told them how sad and miserable I had been, but how happy I was now.

I tried to encourage Tomiko-san as much as possible. When they were leaving, I invited her to come back and see us. In a few days they did return, and we became good friends.

We saw that she needed to learn how to care for herself as I had done, but before that was possible she would have to have some sort of prosthetic device to help her. Akitoshi, who knew all about government help for the handicapped, explained the services that were available. Tomiko-san was anxious to see them, but her mother was reluctant.

"What would they do?" she asked.

"They'll examine her and fit her with an artificial arm and hooks."

Pain marred her solemn face. "That is what I was afraid they would do. I couldn't stand it. No, we will not go to see them."

Akitoshi was patient but insistent. With such devices, he repeated, Tomiko-san would be able to help herself. She would even be able to live alone.

"It would be too painful for me to see Tomiko have metal hands fastened to her body," the girl's mother replied, shuddering. "Every time I saw them I would think of—of—"

The next time they visited, Akitoshi pressed her once more to allow her daughter to see what help she could get from the government. Finally, when he volunteered to go with them, she agreed. Although Tomiko-san's father was quite wealthy, he was an alcoholic and could not be trusted at such a time. He was sure to be drunk and belligerent. Actually, it had been because of the unhappiness and trouble his drinking brought to their home that Tomiko had attempted to take her life.

The men in the government center were understanding and helpful. She was fitted with an artificial arm which was attached to her body by a severe body-length corset and a hook on her stump. Now it was up to her to master the fundamentals they had taught her for using them.

Akitoshi and I had been considering the time when she would have some means of helping herself and trying to figure out what we could do to get her started. She was still as sad and as listless as ever, as devoid of interest in learning to care for herself as she had been the first time she was at our home.

"You're not going to be able to do anything for her unless you can get her away from her mother," he said. "She's being smothered."

When they came to see us once more, I tried to ignite a spark of interest. "Aren't you excited, Tomiko-san? You're soon going to be able to comb your own hair and feed yourself."

Her lips quivered. "How can I? I can't even drink tea unless Mother gives it to me with a spoon like a baby. Everything I need has to be done for me."

I was angry with both of them. "You don't have to use a spoon. And you don't have to pick up the cup unless you want to. Why don't you use a straw?"

Her mother was ready to leap to her daughter's defense, but Tomiko-san's expression changed to incredulity. "I'd never thought of doing it that way."

I tried to explain that now that she had the means of helping herself, this was the way she had to think. Every single thing she wanted to do would have to be grappled with. She would have to figure out different ways of doing each step of each new chore. It wouldn't be easy. She would have so much trouble she would probably have to determine that she was not going to stop until she learned exactly how to do all of the things she would have to do to take care of herself.

She began to look as though she was willing to try. That was what I had been waiting for. I suggested that she come and stay with us for a few days. That was Akitoshi's plan, and it sounded good to me. We had to separate her from her mother. Although the girl was anxious to stay with us, her mother was not sure it would be wise.

"We have never been apart a single night since she was released from the hospital," she said, talking as though Tomiko-san was too young or too ignorant to understand. "I have fed her every bite of food she has eaten. I have undressed her every time she has gone to bed. I've helped her go to the toilet and bathe. I'm afraid it will be too much for you to help her the way I do."

She was really saying she didn't think I could take care of her daughter—that Tomiko-san needed her too much—but she wasn't quite honest or brave enough to put the truth into words.

"We'll get along," I assured her.

Reluctantly she agreed to leave her daughter with us for a few days. "But you will take good care of her, won't you?" she asked pathetically. "Tomiko is so helpless. You will have to do everything for her."

As soon as she was gone, the girl's education began. "I have to go to the toilet," she told me.

"I'll show you how to help yourself."

"But I can't."

"You've never tried."

When she saw I intended to make her help herself, she panicked. "No! I can't do it! I've never done it by myself!"

I tried to reason with her, but it seemed useless. The more I talked, the more certain she was that she could do nothing for herself. Her mother wasn't cruel to her.

I didn't like to be so stern and hard. My heart went out to the bewildered girl beside me. I knew the agony she was experiencing. I had gone through it myself. But I had to make her willing to put forth the effort to become independent.

"Tomiko-san!" I said firmly. "Don't talk that way! Don't even think that way! You *can* learn to help yourself. Make up your mind to that!"

Her lips quivered, and she was close to tears.

"I'm going in with you and I'm going to stay with you until you learn. I know you can do it."

"With these?" she asked piteously, holding out the hooks she had to use in the place of hands.

I had tried an artificial arm several years before and had given up on it because it was so heavy and cumbersome, so I I could understand her feelings. Still, I did not dare let my sympathy show. She had reached a crisis point. She could go on to achieve a large measure of independence, or she could be doomed to a life of helplessness. If she was allowed to give up now, she would be beaten. I loved her too much to allow that. Silently I prayed for guidance and courage to say and do the right things.

"With those." My voice was cold and impersonal. "Come on."

I don't remember exactly how long we stayed in there or how we managed to figure out a way she could dress herself, but she did. God gave me the patience and her the confidence and determination to follow our fumbling directives.

Finally she succeeded. "I can do it!" she shouted. "I can dress myself!"

In the other room Akitoshi heard her and added his prayers of thanksgiving to mine. He was thinking not only of her physical and mental welfare but her soul. He prayed that this might prove to be the opening wedge to allow us to share the Gospel of the Lord Jesus Christ with her and her family.

That first victory was exactly what she needed. The tension drained from her sad face, and hope began to glimmer faintly in her eyes. If you have never been completely dependent on others as an adult, you cannot understand the exhilaration she felt at being able to do this small thing for herself.

This meant more to Tomiko than simply being able to dress without help. Far more. Since her attempted suicide she had believed what her distraught mother told her: that she was helpless and could not be expected to do anything. In her anguish, her mother had tried to make it up to her by waiting on her ceaselessly. My own mother would have done the same. She didn't realize her daughter was growing to hate herself for her helpless condition. She could only guess how bleak the future was to Tomiko. All the girl could look forward to was being a burden on those who loved her. That was the source of much of her sadness.

Now there was hope.

For the first time since the accident, the girl was able to dress herself. If she could do that, she could learn to feed herself and cook and clean the same as I had. She would have to learn different methods because our handicaps were different, but she was on the way. Her passive acceptance of her plight was shoved aside by a strong determination to learn to do everything she had been able to do before the loss of her arms.

"You have found ways of taking care of yourself and your home and children, Yoneko," she said, her excitement bubbling. "I can, too."

And learn she did.

During those next thrilling days, working with Tomiko became an exciting game. Every task was a challenge she was confident she could meet. If she failed, she would try again, grimly.

"There is a way for me to do it," she would say. "All I have to do is to learn how."

She asked me how to hold the dishes to wash them. Then, qiuckly, as though she was afraid I would come up with the answer for her, "Don't tell me! Let me work it out by myself!"

At times I gave suggestions, but they were rarely necessary. Her attitude had changed, and with it her entire personality.

She shucked her sadness as a butterfly shucks its cocoon, and there was happiness and joy in her smile. "Can't do" for Tomiko became "can do." And with all the radiance of a child just introduced to the wonderful world of learning, she mastered one skill after another. When her mother apprehensively came back several days later, she was amazed.

"I can't believe it, Tomiko," she said over and over. "I can't believe it." Her eyes filled with tears, and for a time she could not speak.

"We didn't think you could help her in this way," she managed. "We only thought you might be able to get her to accept her—her handicap and not be so sad."

That day we shared Jesus Christ with Tomiko and her mother. They listened but did not receive Christ immediately. It is no small thing for a Japanese to put aside the worship of his ancestors. But before God led us from our place of service in Tokyo to pastor a church in Okinawa, they both became believers. In fact, their entire family, except for the alcoholic father, received Jesus Christ.

With Tomiko and her family, God was cracking the curtain of the future to give us a glimpse of the joy He had for us in serving Him in the months and years to come. And, strangely, He used my attempted suicide and the mangling of my body as the source of the blessing. Only, we were not yet aware of that.

THIRTEEN

The people of Okinawa are different than the Japanese. Anthropologists have propounded various theories that trace the origin of these island people, but most are agreed that their roots range wide, reaching into a number of peoples and blending their various traits, features, and characteristics into a distinct nationality.

The gentle, rounded features and laughing eyes of the Polynesian are stamped indelibly on the faces seen on the streets of Naha, the capital of Okinawa, but no one claims they are the same as the Tahitian or the other South Pacific islanders. There are traces of the sturdy peasant stock of the Korean and the ambitious cleverness of the Chinese in their makeup. Most Japanese would be appalled at the suggestion that our proud blood was involved in any way in molding the characteristics of the despised Okinawans. Yet, it is there, unmistakably. It blends with the Polynesian, the Chinese, and the Korean to make the Okinawan.

Most anthropologists studying Oriental culture eventually make their way to that pleasant island. The language is the same as is found in ancient Japanese writings, which has brought the conviction that in some ways time has stood still on Okinawa. As the people pressed northward, breaking ties, their language changed, but those who remained behind clung to the old way of speaking.

As I said, most Japanese despise the people of Okinawa as members of a well-bred, educated family might despise their illiterate relatives. During the labor migrations to Hawaii and California earlier in the century, the last words most young men heard from their parents was the admonition not to marry an Okinawan. Such thoughtlessness would bring shame and dishonor to the entire family. There has been much less prejudice in recent years, but with many the old stigma has remained. The individual from Okinawa was looked upon as being not quite as good or as wise or as honorable as a Japanese.

Yet, when Akitoshi came home from his first visit to that beautiful little country, he talked a lot about the people and how much he loved them. Once a year he went there for a month with the chairman of the Japanese field of the Far Eastern Gospel Crusade. They visited the churches, preaching and encouraging believers.

"If God calls me to give my life serving a church as a pastor again," he would tell me when he came back from those trips, "I would love to have it be in Okinawa."

I didn't say anything in reply, but I hoped that wouldn't happen. Marie and Ruth were happy and well adjusted in school and in our neighborhood where they had many friends. Both Akitoshi and I were active for the Lord; and, as far as I could see, we were needed there as much as we were in Okinawa. I suppose most women like the security of familiar surroundings and therefore resist change. I was content to stay where we were. I had no desire even to visit the place.

My reluctance to consider Okinawa as a field of service was not because of prejudice. I had never thought about it seriously enough to have any special attitude toward the people. I was willing to go if we were sure God was calling us. That matter had been settled several years earlier. Still, I would much rather have stayed where we were.

That was not to be, however. God had still another move for us. He was beginning to work in Akitoshi's heart, although I did not know about it at the time. On his last trip to Okinawa, Akitoshi learned that one of the churches desperately needed a pastor. They had been praying for months about it, confident that God would send them just the right man.

They came to my husband and asked if he would consider taking the church. He didn't give them an answer immediately, but he began to feel the insistent tug on his heart that he had come to recognize as the leading of the Holy Spirit.

Back home he prayed earnestly that God would lead him. I had been living with him long enough to know something was troubling him, but I waited for him to tell me. It was a long while before he shared those bewildering days with me. At the time, however, he remained silent. He had put out the fleece as Gideon did and asked for a sign so we would know what we should do.

God gave him a verse. "Ye have not chosen me, but I have chosen you, and ordained you, that ye should go and bring forth fruit."*

He asked God to show him that Okinawa was the place we should serve by having someone quote that same verse to him before a certain date. I'm sure no one had quoted it to him for a year or more until that time. A week later he was asked to fill the pulpit in one of the churches near us. Before he spoke, the wife of one of the missionaries gave her testimony. As she shared some of her recent experiences, tears clouded her eyes.

"God has really been speaking to me these past few weeks through the sixteenth verse of the fifteenth chapter of John," she said.

" 'Go and bring forth fruit.' "

Akitoshi was stunned by the dramatic answer to his plea for guidance. The verse rumbled through his head and heart.

"Yes, Lord," he said silently as he got up to speak. "I will go."

*John 15:16.

That night he told me all about it. I lacked his assurance. That troubled me, but it didn't seem to disturb Akitoshi. I'm not sure whether he realized I was torn by my own personal desires as well as my uncertainty as to God's leading.

"We are one in the sight of God," he replied. "And we are dedicated to His service. If he wants us in Okinawa, He will make that fact plain to you too. We will wait for His guidance."

I prayed about it for a long time, but still no answer came. It seemed that the heavens were as tightly closed against my prayers as they were against the rain during the seven years of drought when Joseph was in Egypt. My confusion was growing, but God was beginning to move. We were soon to be faced with a decision that would change the course of our entire lives.

The people of Okinawa had seen my husband but had never seen me. We wrote them suggesting that we could go there in December for a two-week series of meetings. They were so excited about our coming, even for so brief a visit, that they raised the money for our tickets. Akitoshi was silent for a long while after reading their letter.

"You don't realize the sacrifice this represents," he said. "The people are poor. This is money they need for food and clothing."

When we reached the island, there were more than a dozen who had taken time off from their jobs to come and greet us. I soon saw why he loved the people of Okinawa, and especially those in this church. They were mostly laborers and very poor, but their tired, work-seamed faces radiated with the love of Christ. They were all tugging at my heart before the close of the first week.

We learned they had been holding meetings for some time to see how much money they could raise on a regular basis for our support if the Lord should lead us to come and serve among them. This was their problem, they reasoned. They wanted to meet our expenses the way they felt the Lord would have them do.

"How much are you going to give?" they would ask each family. They should have asked, "How much *can* you give?" That was where the matter really stood. They were people who needed all they could earn to support their families.

The total they arrived at was so small that they felt they could not ask us to come and live on it. So they went back to those same people to see if they could manage to squeeze any more from their income to help support a pastor.

"We know what it will cost a pastor to live here in Okinawa," they said. "We will offer them that much and trust God to supply the rest."

The leaders of the congregation talked to us. We could live in the house they were using as a church, they said. And in addition to the rent, they would give us the equivalent of fifty American dollars a month. That wasn't much, even by our modest standard of living.

I was still not sure God was directing us to move. I was not concerned about the amount of money we would be receiving. We had seen enough of His loving care to know He would see that we had what we needed wherever we were. And it didn't disturb me that the group was small and struggling. Anyone who has served Christ in our part of the world soon becomes accustomed to working with small groups of people and living on sparse checks. Part of my concern was personal. I admitted that and battled against it on my knees as I continued to pray for the Lord's leading.

There was one incident after our first meeting in the church that spoke to my heart. A wizened, arthritic old woman hobbled up to me. When we got better acquainted with the people, I learned she was only in her fifties, but sin and the rigors of eking out a miserable existence had aged her until she looked to be at least eighty. She had been a sorcerer before she received Christ as her Saviour, and she could not read or write. Still, I don't believe I have ever met a more saintly woman.

"I don't have very much money, Mrs. Tahara," she said, "and I can no longer work very hard. But I do have a good garden. The Lord has provided that for me. When you come to help us, I am going to bring you many green vegetables. I will see that you have green vegetables every day."

Looking down into those tender, loving eyes, I felt I could give the rest of my life to this dear lady and the others like her. That spoke to me as nothing else could. Before we went home we were committed to take over the little church at Naha, Okinawa. I've never asked Akitoshi, but I have often wondered if he used those special meetings as an excuse to get me to Okinawa so I could be touched by the love and friendliness of those dear believers.

As soon as we knew we were going there, the people started praying for an air-conditioner for us. The climate was warm and humid the year round, without cooling off at night. It was hard for anyone to get used to such unrelenting heat. The problem was particularly difficult for me.

I hadn't been aware of it until after my accident, but the arms and legs of a person serve much the same purpose as the cooling system of a car. The blood is cooled as it passes through the capillaries and the veins. This helps to keep the average person more comfortable in excessive heat. But I had lost an arm and parts of both legs. My temperature is always a bit higher than normal. Because my cooling system is impaired, I suffer a great deal in hot weather.

The missionaries knew of my problem as well as the situation of the people in the church: that no more of our support could come locally. So the missionaries got us an air-conditioner that cost $280.00. How I thanked God for it.

Before we left Tokyo, we gave our old refrigerator, sewing machine, and washer to some of our friends. We didn't feel we had the money to freight them to our new field of service or that they were worth the cost of shipping. But I was troubled by the decision. I had grown accustomed to those appliances. If we had sold our old ones, we would at least have had a little money to apply on replacements.

"We couldn't have sold them our stuff," my husband told me. "They don't have any extra money for appliances, and they really need them."

"But what are we going to do?" I was thinking of trying to keep food in hot, humid, semitropical Okinawa without refrigeration; of doing our washing without a machine, and of trying to keep two growing daughters in clothes by sewing for them by hand.

"God will work things out for us."

I knew God had undertaken for us on other occasions, and I had learned much about trusting Him. Still, He had a lesson to teach me. He was going to provide, but He allowed me to make what I felt was a sacrifice and reach the place where my resentment was gone. Then He began to fit the pieces into place.

For several months after we started to serve the church in Okinawa, I managed without the machines I had found so helpful in keeping house. Then one of the other churches in Naha was having an American navy chaplain speak to them and asked Akitoshi to interpret. We got acquainted with Commander Hathaway, who was very friendly to both of us. At Christmas he came to our home with a refrigerator, an automatic washer, and several smaller appliances. They were far better than what we had given away. Again God showed me we didn't have to worry. He would take care of us.

I shall never forget our arrival in Okinawa. Everyone in the church must have come down to greet us. We thought some of them would wait and go with us to the old house we would be living in, but nobody did. We both remarked about it.

Then we reached the house and went in. The instant the door swung open we knew the reason for their disappearance. The interior of the old house had been completely redone. The paper partitions were new, and there were new tatami mats on the floor. A lovely meal was on the table ready for us to eat.

"We knew you would be hungry," smiling ladies from the church told us, "so we hurried ahead to prepare dinner for you."

That was to be the pattern of our entire four years in Okianwa. Those dear, gracious people were constantly thinking of ways to please us and make life a bit more comfortable for us. They sacrificed so much for us that at times I felt as David must have when his faithful men risked death to get water from his favorite well for him. Of course we knew they weren't doing it for us. They were doing it because of their love for Jesus Christ.

When we went to the capital of Okinawa with its 300,000 people, there were fifteen to twenty Christians, not counting the children. And they were supporting us at great personal sacrifice. When we left after four years, the Sunday school had reached 150, the church had almost doubled in size to thirty members, and God had blessed financially. They were supporting their pastor and his family and partially supporting Bible school students. They were still poor and still had to make sacrifices to meet their commitments, but God continued to work among them.

While we were still in Japan, Akitoshi got acquainted with the Japanese director of the World Literature Crusade. He knew little literature distribution was being done in Okinawa and was concerned about it. Yes, something could be done, he was told, providing the Japanese believers would underwrite the cost. There was nothing in the budget of the worldwide organization for Okinawa.

Others took the responsibility of raising the funds, but there was no one to write the special tracts that were needed. Akitoshi approached a number of individuals he considered to be qualified, but none would do it.

"Why don't you write the tract?" I asked him.

"It looks as though I'll have to."

I didn't know he was capable of writing so well, or perhaps God gave him special guidance, but the tract was well received by the people. It wasn't too difficult to get tracts distributed or the correspondence courses sent out, but getting the lessons corrected was another matter. Those who would acknowledge that they were qualified for the job were so busy they couldn't help. Or, so they said.

"What are we going to do?" he asked me.

I had an uneasy feeling that he was leading up to something. "We're busy, too," I reminded him.

"But these lessons are the heart of the whole project."

When we started praying that God would give me the strength and time to correct 500 to 600 correspondence courses, it seemed that He would have to increase the length of my day, as He did for a sign to Hezekiah,† if I were to add that task to my other duties. Although He didn't command the sun to move backward for me, the effect was the same. Somehow I was able to get the correspondence courses corrected and enjoyed doing it. It is marvelous what we can accomplish when the Lord is guiding.

Marie and Ruth had much more difficulty adjusting to Okinawa than Akitoshi and I. The schools the girls attended

†See 2 Kings 20:8-11.

in Japan were excellent. Even the students from the poorest of families were scrubbed clean and were respectful and obedient. The teachers were refined and had a concern for their classes.

In Okinawa both girls were shocked when they saw how many of their classmates came in dirty clothes and with grimy hands and faces. They were even more shocked to hear the coarse and even vulgar talk and to see that most classes were completely undisciplined.

And the teachers.

Marie came home one day, crying. She was always tenderhearted.

"Do you know what our teacher told one of the boys today, Mama? He said, 'If you do that again, I'll kill you.'" Her tearstained face came up to look into my eyes. "Do you think he really would?"

She had never heard that sort of talk before, and especially not by a teacher.

However, Ruth's problem was even greater. There was a boy in her division of the fifth grade‡ who constantly tormented her. Every day he humiliated her in some new way. He pulled her hair or ridiculed her in front of the others. He would grab her book bag and open it, showing its contents gleefully to the other boys. Or he would grab her assignment paper and refuse to give it back. He teased her until she began to hate school.

At first we had difficulty understanding the change that had come over our youngest daughter. She had always seemed to enjoy school before. Now she didn't want to go. At first she wouldn't tell us the reason; but when we pressed her, she told us what he had done. After praying about it, Akitoshi decided to go to the teacher with the problem, and arrangements were made to put Ruth in another class.

‡There were several different classes in each grade.

Before she was to be moved, however, God intervened. The subject came up during our devotions, and Ruth acknowledged that she, too, had been at fault.

"I really haven't tried to be nice to him," she said. "I'm sure I haven't treated him the way Jesus would want me to."

"Maybe this is the problem," Akitoshi said. "Perhaps this boy wants to be friends with you and does such things in an effort to get you to notice him."

Ruth couldn't quite understand that; but Akitoshi told her that, even though the things the boy did weren't nice, she still should love him. The next day she went to him and told him she was sorry because she hadn't been kind.

His entire attitude changed. "I did all those things because I wanted you to be my friend," he said. "I have no friends."

He never bothered her again.

I'm sure Ruth or her older sister never reached the place where they preferred the schools in Okinawa to what they were used to in Japan, but they did learn to accept the situation and to get along with those who thought differently than they did.

Back in Japan, Ken Anderson of Ken Anderson films was trying to find a Japanese Christian who was concerned about the ministry of getting Japanese sound tracks made for Christian films. At the time, he had never heard of us, nor had we heard of him, but God was moving. He was about to launch Akitoshi and me into an entirely different ministry that was to span the ocean to America and reach around the world, wherever Japanese is spoken. It was the ministry God had been preparing us for ever since He touched our hearts and brought us to Himself.

FOURTEEN

Ken Anderson was disappointed in the response he was getting from Christians in Japan. They liked the films and thought it would be helpful to have them available in the Japanese language, but the cost frightened them. Always ultraconservative in anything that had to do with finances, they didn't believe it would be possible to provide the money. No one even wanted to try.

Eventually Anderson came to Okinawa, where he approached the acting director of a Christian missionary radio station and voiced his desire. Mr. Austin agreed to get a group together, and Akitoshi was one of them.

God had been preparing my husband for that meeting. A certain uneasiness had taken hold of him. He still loved the people in our church and found satisfaction in preaching, but he was beginning to wonder if God had something entirely different for us. We both prayed much about it, but without mentioning it to Marie and Ruth. We didn't want them to start thinking about a move until we were sure.

Still, we had no thought that God's timetable was coming up "go" for us as Akitoshi went to the radio station to meet Mr. Anderson and see his films. The visitor from America handed Akitoshi his card with a few words printed in small letters at the top.

"If not I, who? If not now, when?"

They burned into my husband's consciousness and in the days that followed were never far from his mind. Later God used them to push us from our little Okinawan church into strange places and among unfamiliar people on the other side of the Pacific.

The men who gathered at the radio station to see the films for review were deeply stirred by them and were quick to see how effective they could be in reaching our people for Christ. After a round of questions, most of which were asked by Akitoshi, the Japanese believers in the little room were eager to have good films available in our language.

However, Akitoshi completely misunderstood the purpose of the meeting. He thought Mr. Anderson was looking for people to hire. He didn't know what the stocky American was trying to accomplish beyond getting Japanese sound tracks made for two or three films. He knew he wasn't interested in working for anybody, for he already had a full-time job serving the Lord. But he had a strong feeling that this American should meet me. At the time he wasn't sure why.

"Yoneko has a wonderful story I think you should hear," he told him.

Anderson was gracious but evasive and noncommittal. He would be glad to meet me and listen to my story, but his interest was only casual. Akitoshi saw by his attitude that he didn't want to get us excited about the possibility of having our story filmed. Later, in public meetings in America, we heard him give his version of the incident.

"When Andy approached me, I wondered how I could be kind and still not give false hopes. Everywhere I go people approach me with stories they think would make the greatest film since *Ben Hur* or *The Ten Commandments.*

" 'You've got to meet these people,' they say. 'They've got this wonderful story. It's really great!'

"And usually it is a wonderful story—to them. Unfortunately, there are certain elements of suspense and motivation and excitement that must be in a story in order to make a good film. So I usually shudder when strangers approach me.

"Frankly, I thought Andy was another one. I went out to their home to hear what I expected to be a very boring account of his wife's life. Instead, it was one of the most thrilling stories I have ever heard."

I didn't know what he was thinking at the time he came out to our house for tea. If I had, I might have been reluctant to share my experiences, and I'm sure Akitoshi would have found his lips closed. But God wanted my story told, so He brought Ken Anderson to us.

I shall never forget the look on his face as my husband interpreted for me. Mr. Anderson's eyes gleamed, and he leaned forward, intent on catching every word of the unfolding narrative.

"Incredible," he murmured. "Fantastic!"

I don't mean to brag. That was his reaction.

When I finished, he had already decided the story had definite film possibilities. We didn't know whether to get excited about it or not. He had not been too encouraging as to the final outcome of the project. He didn't even know whether he would be able to interest investors in it.

He wrote a short synopsis of my story and had it duplicated and sent to his distributors. Their reaction was far from encouraging. They thought it interesting, but there were questions in their minds as to the use American churches would make of such a film. A year or so later, a Christian doctor* who was working in India made funds available for producing the film *Yoneko.*

But before that happened, Akitoshi was deeply involved with International Films,† translating the sound track of two films into Japanese. The more he worked, the stronger became the conviction that he should be working full time in

*Dr. Geoffrey Lehmen, the subject of *Himalayan Heartbeat* by Ken Anderson.

†The nonprofit missionary arm of Ken Anderson films.

films. When we were sure this was God's doing, he went to tell the American missionary and arranged a meeting with five or six of the church leaders. They had no inkling that we were even considering a move, and the news stunned them, but they accepted it beautifully.

"I know God has blessed you with special gifts, Tahara-sensei," one of the men said. "We're not mainly concerned with having more people in our church. We want to work with everybody else to help save souls for the Lord."

"We need a pastor for our church," one of the others told him, "but you are free to go. We believe the Lord is calling you, and we want you to be obedient to Him."

Before we left, they told us they would like to support us but did not have the money. We knew that well. They were extending themselves beyond their capabilities by assuming the support of a pastor.

"You will be our missionary in Christian films," an elderly man told Akitoshi. "We will uphold you with our prayers."

After we made our decision to enter the film ministry, Ken Anderson asked my husband to accompany him as a recording technician on a trip to Vietnam to film *The Peacemakers.*

"I can't pay you for it, Andy," he said. "There was no allowance in the budget for a sound man, but we will take care of your transportation and expenses."

He was away for a month. His education in the making of films had begun.

When the time came for the shooting of *Yoneko,* we resigned from our church and left Okinawa. That was one of the saddest days of our lives.

"We will be back," we told the people in an effort to comfort them and stop their weeping. But everyone knew it would never be the same.

When the film was shot and only the editing remained, Ken Anderson asked us if we would like to go to the States to promote *Yoneko,* learn more about film-making, and broaden our base of missionary support.

I would honestly have rather stayed in Japan, but I knew this time that there was no question about the leading of the Lord. So once again we headed for a new ministry in a new location. We were launching into the work God had been training us for. This was to be our ministry: preparing Christian films for use in Japan.

We soon learned that *Yoneko* was to have a far greater ministry than we had anticipated. In Japan, where suicide is always a problem, especially among the young, it has been widely acclaimed. Despondent young men and women who were considering the course I tried have drawn new courage to go on living because they saw the film. Hungry hearts have been fed and souls saved.

And in America we were thrilled to see the response when we showed the film. Usually we would screen the film, then I would speak, with Akitoshi interpreting. We saw many saved and made hundreds of new American friends.

Now we are back in Japan where Akitoshi is working with International Films. We are confidently looking forward to the future, knowing God has even wider horizons, even greater avenues of service, for us. How thankful I am to Him that He was concerned enough about me to keep me from destroying myself and tenderly leading me to Christ and then to a place of total commitment.

That is why our daughters have never seen me cry because of what happened. Had I not thrown myself under the train that night at Shinjuku Station, I probably would never have put my trust in Jesus Christ to save me.

That is the reason I have become the kind of person my name predicted. It is because of God and His loving, watchful guidance and care that I am Yoneko—rice child—daughter of happiness.